foolproof CRAZY QUILTING

Visual Guide—25 Stitch Maps
100+ Embroidery & Embellishment Stitches

JENNIFER CLOUSTON

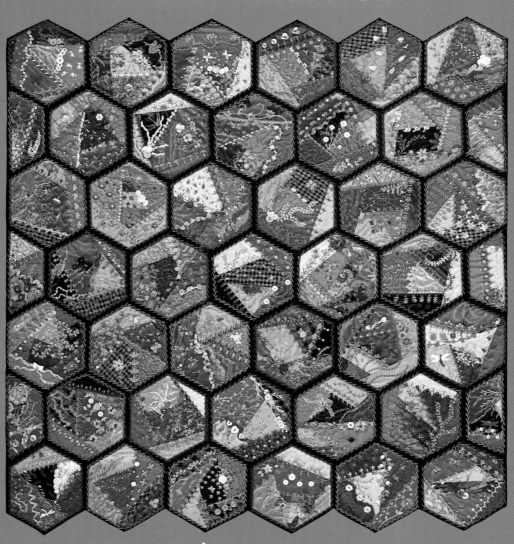

C&T PUBLISHING

Text copyright © 2013 by Jennifer Clouston

Photography and Artwork copyright © 2013 by C&T Publishing, Inc.

Publisher: Amy Marson

Creative Director: Gailen Runge

Art Director: Kristy Zacharias

Editor: Liz Aneloski

Technical Editors: Julie Waldman and Gailen Runge

Cover Designers: Kristen Yenche and Kristy Zacharias

Book Designer: April Mostek

Production Coordinators: Jessica Jenkins, Jenny Davis, and Zinnia Heinzmann

Production Editors: Alice Mace Nakanishi and Katie Van Amburg

Illustrator: Mary E. Flynn

Photography by Diane Pedersen and Nissa Brehmer of C&T Publishing, Inc., unless otherwise noted

Published by C&T Publishing, Inc., P.O. Box 1456, Lafayette, CA 94549

Library of Congress Cataloging-in-Publication Data

Clouston, Jennifer, 1959-

Foolproof crazy quilting : visual guide--25 stitch maps - 100+ embroidery & embellishment stitches / Jennifer Clouston.

    pages cm

ISBN 978-1-60705-717-8 (soft cover)

1. Patchwork--Patterns. 2. Crazy quilts. 3. Stitches (Sewing) I. Title.

TT835.C599 2013

746.46--dc23

                    2013013791

Printed in China

10 9 8 7 6 5 4 3 2 1

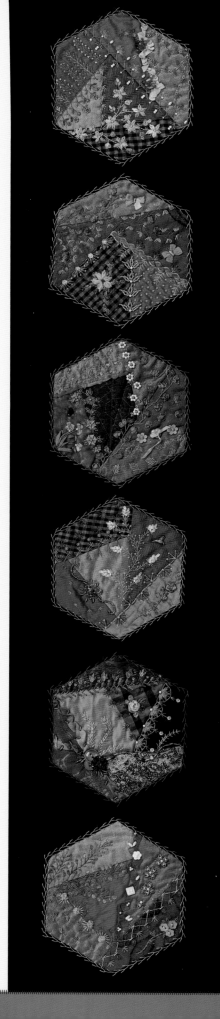

Dedication

Foolproof Crazy Quilting
is dedicated to the memory
of my late sister, Carol.

Acknowledgments

"No man is an island" is one of my favorite quotes. It goes without saying that human beings do not thrive when isolated from others. My book has come to fruition as a result of the people I share my life with:

My husband, Vaughn, without whom I could not have written this book. Your patience with my computer illiteracy and your hours spent at the computer are invaluable to me. Thank you! Thank you! Thank you!

My children, Gareth and Ainslie, who have grown up with their mom sewing and have always taken an interest in the work I create, both critiquing and encouraging.

My beloved parents, David and Penny, who have offered unconditional love, for each other and their children.

My brother, Jonathan, who deserves a big thank-you for fine-tuning my ramblings.

My late sister, Carol, who is looking down on me with pride and joy. Of that I am certain.

My grandmother, who lovingly taught me how to knit, crochet, and sew.

The teachers who taught me in the beginning stages of my quilting journey, especially Dianne Sturgess, my first patchwork teacher, who became a lifelong friend.

Rosalie Dace, who introduced me to crazy quilting.

My friends, who encouraged me to write this book and continued the encouragement throughout the process.

Last but not least, the women that I have been fortunate enough to teach. Together we have shared more than the stitch combinations and cups of tea.

In closing, a big thank-you to the people at C&T Publishing, who believed I could do it!

Contents

I was very fortunate to grow up in South Africa. Her colors, landscapes, people, and many cultures formed an incredible backdrop to my childhood.

African art

I had a wonderful grandmother who taught me how to knit, crochet, and sew. She took me to the Indian markets during a time in apartheid South Africa when it was taboo. The images of heaped spices, lovely saris, and shiny sequins have stayed with me all my life.

Indian-market influences

I went to my first patchwork class with Dianne Sturgess in the 1980s, and I was hooked. A few years later, Rosalie Dace introduced me to crazy quilting. It was in crazy quilting that I found an outlet for my love of embroidery, color, and beading. The beadwork of the Zulu and the colors of the Indian communities in Natal have heavily influenced my work.

Indian embroidery

Zulu beadwork

Crazy quilting is a gentle art that has given me years of pleasure and entertainment. I have taken the traditions of Victorian crazy quilting and fused them with my South African influences to create my own style of crazy quilting.

We all have our own stitch "fingerprint" and our personal taste in color, fabrics, and style. It is my wish that *Foolproof Crazy Quilting* will stimulate your imagination while at the same time encouraging you to stay true to your own unique influences and artistic flair.

2 A Brief History of Crazy Quilting

Artwork reflects, and is influenced by, the world around us. Today's crazy quilting is influenced by the highly embroidered and embellished style of patchwork that reached its peak toward the end of the Victorian era.

The late nineteenth century was a time of great change. Queen Victoria was an avid believer in embracing the "New World." England was being exposed to new cultures and people. Never-before-seen fabrics, spices, food, fauna, and flora were the new status symbols. It was a sign of wealth and prosperity to be seen with all the trappings of the New World. In addition, as the queen, and England, were coming out of their long period of mourning for their beloved Albert, dark and somber fashions in both clothing and interior decorating made way for color.

The Industrial Revolution, too, was in full swing. A lot of money was being made, and a new class was emerging—the nouveau riche. The wealthy Victorian woman, however, was largely thought of as little more than a decoration on the arm of her husband. She was educated only to a point of basic reading and writing. As a show of wealth and refinement, she would have housekeepers, cooks, butlers, housemaids, gardeners, and nannies at her beck and call, yet little or no say in her own life or aspirations.

One of the skills she was expected to excel in, as this too was a symbol of refinement and status, was needlework. More than a status symbol, though, needlework came to be an avenue for women to express themselves in a dramatic way. The skills learned while creating structured and precise samplers were now showcased in vividly colored and embellished quilts. The luscious new fabrics from the East and a variety of threads, trinkets, bold colors, and keepsakes were now being incorporated into women's previously demure needlework.

The initial view of this new "garish" or "crazy" work was soon to change. A crazy quilt, holding pride of place, draped over the grand piano in the main room, was now a symbol of wealth and status, indicating a life of luxury—for surely to produce work of such magnitude must take an enormous amount of time, which only the wealthiest women would have at their disposal.

The crazy quilt star shone brightly for only a short period of time. Toward the end of the nineteenth century, life and attitudes were changing. Within a couple of decades women would be allowed to vote, skirts would become shorter, and women would want more from their lives. By 1914 the world would be plunged into war and would never be the same. By the end of the 1920s, the crazy quilt fad had faded.

Today, though, crazy quilting is enjoying a resurgence in popularity. With a plentitude of threads, fabrics, beads, and trims at our disposal, the crazy quilts of today have taken on a more contemporary look.

While crazy quilting is time consuming and, in some respects, a little indulgent, it is a perfect way to find calm in our busy lives.

Choosing Fabrics and Foundation Piecing

Choosing Fabrics

Victorian women used a large variety of fabrics in crazy quilts: brocades, silks, satins, fine woolens, taffetas. The colors reflected the fashions of the time. Likewise, your choice of fabric will reflect what you have on hand. I encourage you to be brave with your choice of color and fabric type—use any fabric that appeals to you. There are some fabric types that may be a challenge to use, but if you love them, there are ways you can make them work.

A few things to remember when choosing fabrics:

- Embroidery and embellishing is what you want to showcase, so it is important to use highly patterned fabrics sparingly.

Too many patterned fabrics

- Try to incorporate a large variety of fabric textures.

- Do not mix "muddy" colors with "clear" colors.

- Use only one genre of fabric—if you are using modern "fresh" fabrics, use them throughout the project.

- If there is one color that stands out too much, make sure to include that color in the embroidery threads and embellishments, thereby diluting it.

- Be aware that high-nap fabrics (such as velvets) are not conducive to flat seams.

Foundation Piecing

There are many piecing techniques that can be used in crazy quilting; however, I use the foundation method. The geometric shapes allow me the freedom to go "crazy" with my seam treatments without losing the shapes of the pieces within the block.

I use prewashed muslin as the foundation fabric, although any neutral fabric is suitable. A low thread count ensures that the delicate embroidery threads and silk ribbons do not wear out too quickly as they pass through the layers of fabric. The foundation fabric gives strength to fine fabrics and a firm base for heavy embellishments such as button clusters.

Requirements for Each Crazy Hexagon

- 12″ × 12″ square of muslin

- 5–6 pieces of interesting fabrics, approximately 5″ × 8″

- Freezer paper

- Hera marker or pencil

- Ruler

- Rotary cutter and mat

- Sewing machine and a neutral-colored thread

- Iron and ironing board

- Appliqué mat (a nonstick pressing sheet), Silicone Release Paper (by C&T Publishing), or parchment baking paper

Method

1. Trace your chosen hexagon pattern (pages 101–110) on the matte (dull) side of the freezer paper, and number all of the shapes with both the hexagon number and the piece number.

2. Cut out the shapes from freezer paper—these shapes are the templates, and they can be reused.

3. Center and trace the hexagon pattern and numbering onto the muslin square; there will be approximately 3″ of muslin around the edge of the hexagon shape.

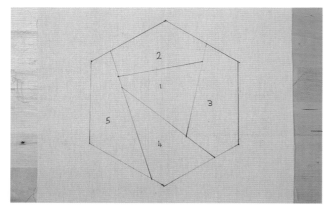

Trace hexagon design onto muslin.

4. Select the fabrics.

5. Place the shiny side of the freezer paper on the right side of the fabric and press without steam. Freezer paper is slightly translucent, so you can easily fussy cut the fabric, if desired.

6. Cut out the shapes, adding a ½″ seam allowance.

Place freezer-paper template on right side of fabric.

7. Stitch along the outside line of the marked hexagon shape on the muslin.

8. Place the muslin with its marked side up, and lay piece 1 over area 1 on the muslin; the perimeter lines of area 1 should be covered by the fabric. Remove the freezer paper (it can be used many times).

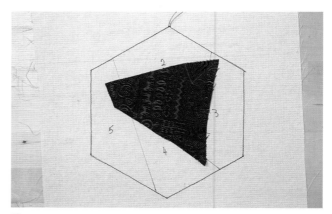

Place piece 1 over area 1.

9. Lay piece 2, right side down, on piece 1, making sure that when it is stitched, flipped, and pressed, the perimeter lines of area 2 on the muslin will be covered by the fabric.

10. Align a ruler on the adjoining line between pieces 1 and 2, and score the fabric with a Hera marker (or mark with a pencil). This is the stitching line.

tip

To help align the ruler on the line, lift the fabric slightly until the pencil line is visible.

Lift fabric until pencil line is visible.

11. Pin and stitch ½″ beyond the neighboring lines.

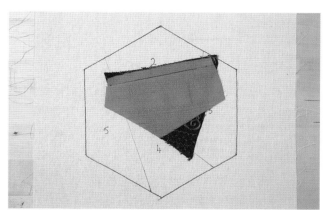

Pin and stitch.

12. Flip piece 2 open and press well. It is very important to keep the work flat during this process.

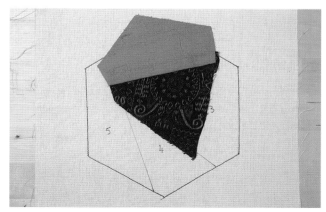

Flip and press.

13. Continue adding pieces in numbered order until the hexagon is complete.

tip

Use a pressing sheet or a sheet of parchment paper while pressing to prevent the fabrics from scorching.

14. Press well.

15. Place the hexagon wrong side up and sew over the perimeter line of the hexagon you stitched in Step 7.

Completed hexagon

16. To form a half-hexagon, complete the steps above using the half-hexagon pattern (page 101).

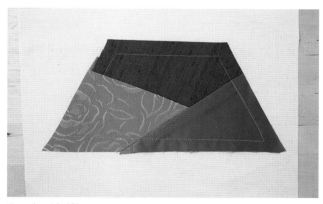

Completed half-hexagon

Basic Sewing Supplies

- Small pair of scissors

- Embroidery hoop

- Marking pencil (The erasable Sewline Trio is my marking pencil of choice.)

- Thimble

- Thread Heaven (I find this thread conditioner and protectant product particularly helpful when working with metallic threads.)

- Desktop, daylight light

tip

A vintage pipe stand works well as a scissor and thimble keeper.

Vintage pipe stand

Needles

There are many types and brands of needles. I prefer to keep the number of needles I work with to a minimum. My brand of choice is Bohin.

- Milliners #4 and #7 for all-around work

- Milliners #10 for the majority of beading

- Beading #12 for beaded backstitch and for very small beads

- Chenille #22 for silk ribbon, twisted silk, twisted rayon, and metallic threads

A chenille needle is a thicker needle with a large eye that allows difficult and delicate threads to pass through the many layers of fabric without getting damaged.

I use a small pincushion to keep my needles in one place.

Threads

There are so many threads available to us. Basically, if a thread can go through the eye of a needle and the layers of fabric, it may be used in crazy quilting. For the purposes of this book, I have used threads that are available at most sewing supply stores.

That said, stranded cotton is not my thread of choice. I much prefer to use perle cotton #8 and #12; since it is a twisted thread, it has a higher loft and a better sheen than stranded cotton.

Perle cotton #8 thread

Rayon threads add sheen and vibrancy to crazy quilting. They do, however, tangle easily. To avoid tangling, press the thread well with a hot steam iron and work with a chenille #22 needle.

Twisted rayon thread

Twisted silk threads are beautiful to work with. Like rayon threads, they are best worked with a chenille #22 needle, which prepares a hole in the fabric, allowing the delicate silk fibers to pass easily through the layers.

Twisted silk thread

Metallic threads are a must for spider webs and insect legs, among other things. Once again, I prefer a chenille #22 needle for metallic threads. Thread Heaven conditioner and protectant works well to settle the fibers of the sometimes prickly metallic threads.

tip

For easy threading, "needle your thread" instead of threading your needle. By this I mean keep the thread still and move the needle onto the thread.

Silk Ribbon

I use a chenille #22 needle with 4mm and 7mm variegated or solid-color silk ribbon. I use a chenille #22 needle with 4mm and 7mm organza ribbon.

Silk ribbon

Beading

I use beading #10–#13 needles and milliners #10 needles with assorted colors of Nymo or Silamide beading thread.

Nymo beading thread

Beads come in an impressive array of shapes, sizes, and colors. Collect as many varieties as possible. Anything with a hole in it can be a bead!

I line a small jar lid with a piece of beading mat or a circle of felt to keep my beads under control.

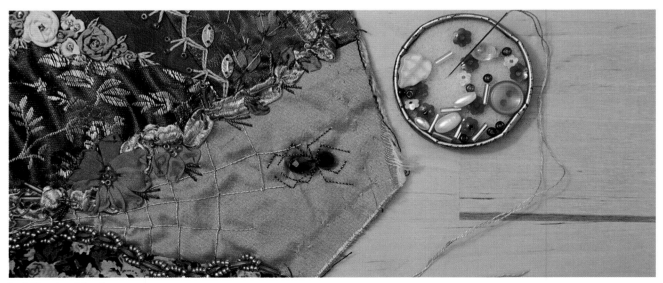

Jar lid lined with beading mat

Embellishing

The options for embellishment materials are endless. Gather keepsakes from grandmothers, lace from baby clothes, and whatever else you can think of—this is an ideal opportunity to display family treasures.

Here are some items you may use:

- All types of lace, trims, and rickrack in an assortment of widths and colors

- Buttons—how we love the humble button!—all shapes and sizes

- Charms: birds, bees, dragonflies, hearts, and so on

- Silk ribbon: 11mm

- Organza ribbon: 7mm

- Coordinating threads

- Milliners #10 needles and beading #12 needles

A few things to keep in mind:

- Try to use a hoop or frame to hold the work taut and flat.

- Crazy quilting is all about the embroidery stitches. If your thread of choice does not show up, change to a different color or texture.

- The size of the embroidery stitches is personal, one aspect of our unique stitch fingerprint.

- It is best to work with a shorter thread—the more often the thread travels through the work, the more it wears. Do not work with worn or frayed thread.

- Some seam treatments are made up of more than one stitch, so it is important not to make that first embroidery stitch too small.

- There are many different marking pens and pencils on the market. But I encourage you to stitch without marking the fabric—this may prove to be frustrating in the beginning, but persevere; the end result will be your own interpretation of the stitch. Unmarked lines allow you the freedom to work to your own stitch fingerprint.

- Variegated threads add color and movement to seam treatments without your having to change the color of thread during a stitch.

- Buttons with shanks do not lie flat on the work.

tip

Crazy quilting materials seem to spread out in a work space. My antique writing desk, fitted with good lighting, works perfectly as my designated stitching area, allowing me the freedom of not having to pack up after each sewing session.

Designated work space

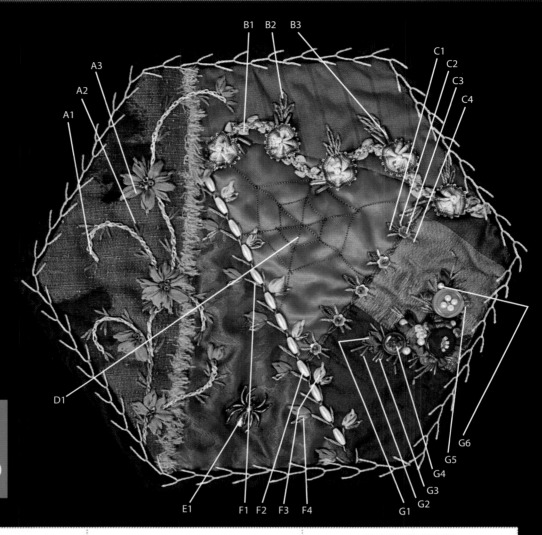

Hexagon 1

(Pattern 1, page 102)

A1

Whipped chain stitch (page 79)

Twisted rayon thread

Chenille #22 needle

A3

Lazy daisy / detached chain stitch flower with seed bead center (page 76)

4mm silk ribbon and Nymo thread

Chenille #22 and milliners #10 needles

B2

Lazy daisy / detached chain stitch (page 72)

Perle cotton #8 thread

Milliners #4 needle

A2

Stab/straight stitch (page 73)

2 strands rayon thread

Milliners #7 needle

B1

Couched braid or trim (page 90)

Nymo thread

Milliners #7 needle

B3

Single-bead stitch (page 85)

Nymo thread

Milliners #10 needle

C1

Lazy daisy / detached chain
stitch (page 72)

3 strands stranded thread

Milliners #7 needle

F1

Fly stitch (page 72)

2 strands rayon thread

Milliners #7 needle

G2

Stab/straight stitch (page 73)

Twisted silk thread

Chenille #22 needle

C2

Stab/straight stitch (page 73)

Stranded rayon thread

Chenille #22 needle

F2

Single-bead stitch (page 85)

Nymo thread

Milliners #10 needle

G3

Stab/straight stitch (page 73)

1 strand rayon thread

Milliners #7 needle

C3

Beaded sequin (page 83)

Nymo thread

Milliners #10 needle

F3

Lazy daisy / detached chain
stitch—silk ribbon (page 76)

4mm silk ribbon

Chenille #22 needle

G4

Simple beaded button (page 91)

Nymo thread

Milliners #10 needle

C4

Stab/straight stitch (page 73)

Twisted silk thread

Chenille #22 needle

F4

Lazy daisy / detached chain
stitch (page 72)

2 strands rayon thread

Milliners #7 needle

G5

Colonial knot (page 71)

Twisted silk thread

Milliners #4 needle

D1

Round spider web (page 88)

Metallic thread

Chenille #22 needle

G1

Ribbon stitch (page 77)

4mm silk ribbon

Chenille #22 needle

G6

Single-bead stitch (page 85)

Nymo thread

Milliners #10 needle

E1

Charm (page 90)

Nymo thread

Milliners #10 needle

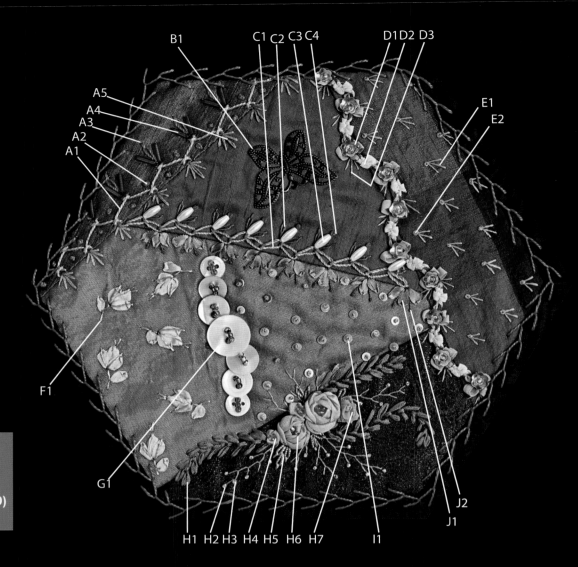

B1
C1 C2 C3 C4
D1 D2 D3
A5
A4
A3
A2
A1
E1
E2
F1
G1
J2
J1
H1 H2 H3 H4 H5 H6 H7
I1

Hexagon 2

(Pattern 9, page 110)

A1

Herringbone stitch (page 72)
Perle cotton #8 thread
Milliners #4 needle

A4

Single-bead stitch (page 85)
Nymo thread
Milliners #10 needle

C1

Zigzag chain stitch (page 74)
Twisted rayon thread
Chenille #22 needle

A2

Colonial knot (page 71)
Perle cotton #8 thread
Milliners #4 needle

A5

Stab/straight stitch (page 73)
2 strands DMC thread
Milliners #7 needle

C2

Lazy daisy/detached chain
stitch (page 72)
1 strand DMC thread
Milliners #7 needle

A3

Lazy daisy/detached chain
stitch (page 72)
Twisted silk thread
Chenille #22 needle

B1

Charm (page 90)
Nymo thread
Milliners #10 needle

C3

Single-bead stitch (page 85)
Nymo thread
Milliners #10 needle

C4

Colonial knot (page 71)
3 strands DMC thread
Milliners #7 needle

D1

Beaded sequin (page 83)
Nymo thread
Milliners #10 needle

D2

Couched braid or trim (page 90)
Nymo thread
Milliners #10 needle

D3

Stab/straight stitch (page 73)
1 strand rayon thread
Milliners #7 needle

E1

Stab/straight stitch (page 73)
1 strand rayon thread
Milliners #7 needle

E2

Colonial knot (page 71)
2 strands rayon thread
Milliners #7 needle

F1

Rosebud (page 88)
4mm silk ribbon and
1 strand rayon thread
Chenille #22 and milliners #7 needles

G1

Simple beaded button (page 91)
Nymo thread
Milliners #10 needle

H1

Fly stitch (page 72)
4mm silk ribbon
Chenille #22 needle

H2

Single-bead stitch (page 85)
Nymo thread
Milliners #10 needle

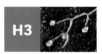

H3

Feather stitch (page 72)
1 strand DMC thread
Milliners #7 needle

H4

Loop stitch with bead (page 76)
7mm silk ribbon and Nymo thread
Chenille #22 and milliners #10 needles

H5

Lazy daisy/detached chain
stitch (page 72)
Twisted silk thread
Chenille #22 needle

H6

Spider web rose with seed
bead center (page 79)
7mm silk ribbon and Nymo thread
Chenille #22 and milliners #10 needles

H7

Ruched rose (page 78)
7mm silk ribbon
Chenille #22 needle

I1

Beaded sequin (page 83)
Nymo thread
Milliners #10 needle

J1

Ribbon stitch (page 77)
4mm silk ribbon
Chenille #22 needle

J2

Pistil stitch (page 73)
1 strand DMC thread
Milliners #7 needle

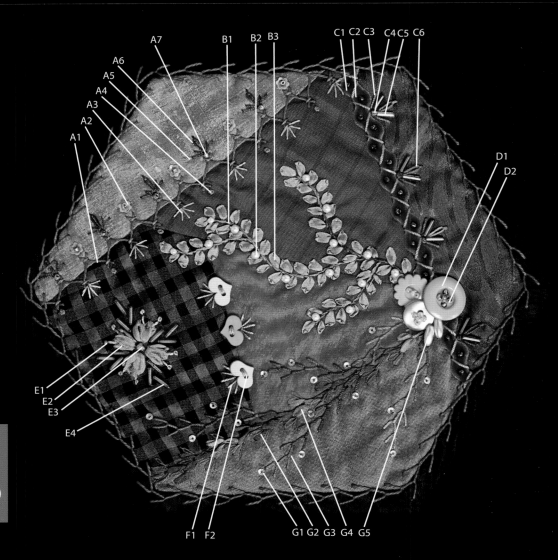

Labels on main image: A1, A2, A3, A4, A5, A6, A7, B1, B2, B3, C1, C2, C3, C4, C5, C6, D1, D2, E1, E2, E3, E4, F1, F2, G1, G2, G3, G4, G5

Hexagon 3

(Pattern 9, page 110)

A1

Herringbone stitch (page 72)
Perle cotton #8 thread
Milliners #4 needle

A2

Beaded sequin (page 83)
Nymo thread
Milliners #10 needle

A3

Stab/straight stitch (page 73)
1 strand rayon thread
Milliners #7 needle

A4

Colonial knot (page 71)
Perle cotton #8 thread
Milliners #4 needle

A5

Stab/straight stitch (page 73)
Twisted silk thread
Chenille #22 needle

A6

Lazy daisy / detached chain
stitch (page 72)
Twisted silk thread
Chenille #22 needle

A7

Single-bead stitch (page 85)
Nymo thread
Milliners #10 needle

B1

Stem stitch (page 73)
3 strands DMC thread
Milliners #7 needle

B2

Single-bead stitch (page 85)
Nymo thread
Milliners #10 needle

B3

Ribbon stitch (page 77)
4mm silk ribbon
Chenille #22 needle

D1

Button cluster (page 90)
Nymo thread
Milliners #10 needle

F2

Button (page 90)
Twisted rayon thread
Milliners #4 needle

C1

Single-bead stitch (page 85)
Nymo thread
Milliners #10 needle

D2

Simple beaded button (page 91)
Nymo thread
Milliners #10 needle

G1

Beaded sequin (page 83)
Nymo thread
Milliners #10 needle

C2

Couched rickrack (page 90)
Twisted rayon thread
Chenille #22 needle

E1

Pistil stitch (page 73)
Twisted silk thread
Milliners #4 needle

G2

Lazy daisy / detached chain
stitch (page 72)
1 strand DMC thread
Milliners #7 needle

C3

Stab/straight stitch (page 73)
Twisted silk thread
Chenille #22 needle

E2

Lazy daisy / detached chain
stitch—silk ribbon (page 76)
4mm silk ribbon
Chenille #22 needle

G3

Feather stitch (page 72)
Twisted silk thread
Chenille #22 needle

C4

Colonial knot (page 71)
Twisted silk thread
Milliners #4 needle

E3

Colonial knot (page 71)
4mm silk ribbon
Chenille #22 needle

G4

Feather stitch (page 72)
4mm silk ribbon
Chenille #22 needle

C5

Single-bead stitch (page 85)
Nymo thread
Milliners #10 needle

E4

Bugle bead leaf (page 83)
Nymo thread
Milliners #10 needle

G5

Single-bead stitch (page 85)
Nymo thread
Milliners #10 needle

C6

Lazy daisy / detached chain
stitch (page 72)
Twisted silk thread
Chenille #22 needle

F1

Stab/straight stitch (page 73)
Perle cotton #8 thread
Milliners #4 needle

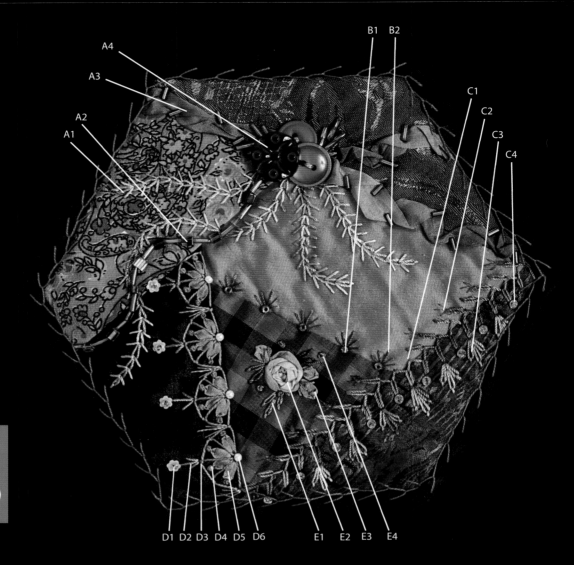

Hexagon 4

(Pattern 7, page 108)

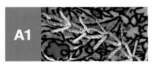

A1
Wheatear stitch (page 73)
Twisted silk thread
Chenille #22 needle

A3
Couched ribbon garland (page 90)
11mm silk ribbon and Nymo thread
Milliners #10 needle

B1
Single-bead stitch (page 85)
Nymo thread
Milliners #10 needle

A2
Beaded backstitch (page 80)
Nymo thread
Beading needle

A4
Button cluster (page 90)
Nymo thread
Milliners #10 needle

B2
Stab/straight stitch (page 73)
Twisted silk thread
Chenille #22 needle

C1

Chain feather stitch (page 71)
Twisted silk thread
Chenille #22 needle

D2

Stab/straight stitch (page 73)
Twisted silk thread
Chenille #22 needle

E1

Lazy daisy/detached chain
stitch (page 72)
Twisted silk thread
Chenille #22 needle

C2

Stab/straight stitch (page 73)
1 strand rayon thread
Milliners #7 needle

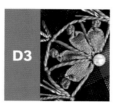

D3

Buttonhole/blanket stitch fan (page 70)
Perle cotton #8 thread
Milliners #4 needle

E2

Spider web rose with seed
bead center (page 79)
7mm silk ribbon and Nymo thread
Chenille #22 and milliners #10 needles

C3

Lazy daisy/detached chain
stitch (page 72)
Twisted silk thread
Chenille #22 needle

D4

Colonial knot (page 71)
Perle cotton #7 thread
Milliners #4 needle

E3

Rosebud (page 88)
4mm silk ribbon and twisted silk thread
Chenille #22 needle

C4

Beaded sequin (page 83)
Nymo thread
Milliners #10 needle

D5

Ribbon stitch (page 77)
4mm silk ribbon
Chenille #22 needle

E4

Colonial knot (page 71)
Twisted silk thread
Milliners #4 needle

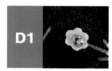

D1

Beaded sequin (page 83)
Nymo thread
Milliners #10 needle

D6

Single-bead stitch (page 85)
Nymo thread
Milliners #10 needle

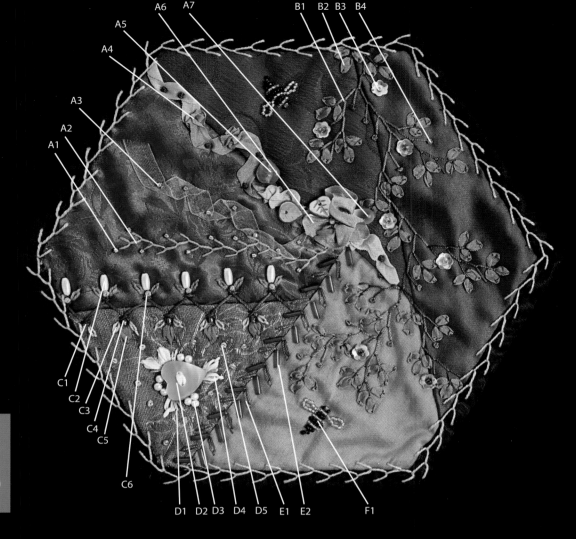

Hexagon 5

(Pattern 4, page 105)

A1

Single-bead stitch (page 85)
Nymo thread
Milliners #10 needle

A2

Feather stitch (page 72)
2 strands DMC thread
Milliners #7 needle

A3

Couched ribbon garland (page 90)
7mm organza ribbon and Nymo thread
Milliners #10 needle

A4

Ruched silk ribbon garland (page 78)
7mm silk ribbon and
1 strand DMC thread
Milliners #10 needle

A5

Single-bead stitch (page 85)
Nymo thread
Milliners #10 needle

A6

Free-form flower with beaded
center (page 91)
11mm silk ribbon and Nymo thread
Milliners #10 needle

A7

Single-bead stitch (page 85)
Nymo thread
Milliners #10 needle

C3

Lazy daisy/detached chain
stitch (page 72)
Perle cotton #8 thread
Milliners #4 needle

D3

Single-bead stitch (page 85)
Nymo thread
Milliners #10 needle

B1

Feather stitch (page 72)
Twisted silk thread
Chenille #22 needle

C4

Single-bead stitch (page 85)
Nymo thread
Milliners #10 needle

D4

Rosebud (page 88)
4mm silk ribbon and twisted silk thread
Chenille #22 needle

B2

Ribbon stitch (page 77)
4mm silk ribbon
Chenille #22 needle

C5

Lazy daisy/detached chain
stitch—silk ribbon (page 76)
4mm silk ribbon
Chenille #22 needle

D5

Colonial knot (page 71)
Twisted silk thread
Milliners #4 needle

B3

Beaded sequin (page 83)
Nymo thread
Milliners #10 needle

C6

Colonial knot (page 71)
Perle cotton #8 thread
Milliners #4 needle

E1

Lazy daisy/detached chain
stitch (page 72)
Twisted silk thread
Chenille #22 needle

B4

Colonial knot (page 71)
Twisted silk thread
Milliners #4 needle

D1

Stab/straight stitch (page 73)
Perle cotton #8 thread
Milliners #4 needle

E2

Single-bead stitch (page 85)
Nymo thread
Milliners #10 needle

C1

Herringbone stitch (page 72)
Twisted silk thread
Chenille #22 needle

D2

Button (page 90)
4mm silk ribbon
Chenille #22 needle

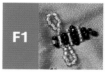

F1

Beaded bee (page 81)
Nymo thread
Beading needle

C2

Single-bead stitch (page 85)
Nymo thread
Milliners #10 needle

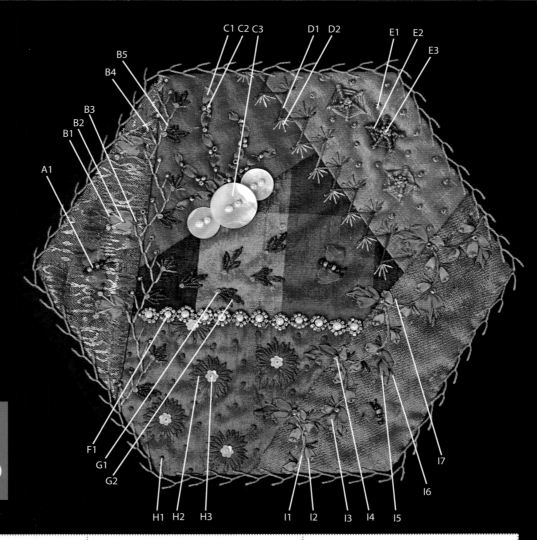

C1 C2 C3 D1 D2 E1 E2 E3
B5
B4
B3
B2
B1
A1
F1
G1
G2
H1 H2 H3 I1 I2 I3 I4 I5 I6 I7

Hexagon 6

(Pattern 2, page 103)

A1

Small beaded bee with organza ribbon wings (page 88)

Nymo thread and 7mm organza ribbon

Chenille #22 and milliners #10 needles

B3

Colonial knot (page 71)

Perle cotton #8 thread

Milliners #4 needle

C1

Ribbon stitch (page 77)

4mm silk ribbon

Chenille #22 needle

B1

Pistil stitch (page 73)

Twisted silk thread

Milliners #4 needle

B4

Single-bead stitch (page 85)

Nymo thread

Milliners #10 needle

C2

Single-bead stitch (page 85)

Nymo thread

Milliners #10 needle

B2

Ribbon stitch (page 77)

4mm silk ribbon

Chenille #22 needle

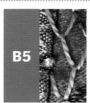

B5

Feather stitch (page 72)

Perle cotton #7 thread

Milliners #4 needle

C3

Single-bead button (page 91)

Nymo thread

Milliners #10 needle

D1

Cretan stitch (page 72)
Twisted silk thread
Chenille #22 needle

G1

Colonial knot (page 71)
Twisted silk thread
Milliners #4 needle

I2

Ribbon stitch (page 77)
4mm silk ribbon
Chenille #22 needle

D2

Stab/straight stitch (page 73)
1 strand rayon thread
Milliners #7 needle

G2

Lazy daisy/detached chain
stitch (page 72)
Twisted silk thread
Chenille #22 needle

I3

Ribbon stitch (page 77)
4mm silk ribbon
Chenille #22 needle

E1

Colonial knot (page 71)
Perle cotton #8 thread
Milliners #4 needle

H1

Colonial knot (page 71)
Perle cotton #12 thread
Milliners #7 needle

I4

Single-bead stitch (page 85)
Nymo thread
Milliners #10 needle

E2

Woven spider web (page 74)
Perle cotton #8 thread
Milliners #4 needle

H2

Lazy daisy/detached chain
stitch (page 72)
Perle cotton #12 thread
Milliners #7 needle

I5

Lazy daisy/detached chain
stitch—silk ribbon (page 76)
4mm silk ribbon
Chenille #22 needle

E3

Beaded sequin (page 83)
Nymo thread
Milliners #10 needle

H3

Beaded sequin (page 83)
Nymo thread
Milliners #10 needle

I6

Stab/straight stitch (page 73)
1 strand rayon thread
Milliners #7 needle

F1

Daisy chain (page 84)
Nymo thread
Beading needle

I1

Stem stitch (page 73)
Perle cotton #12 thread
Milliners #7 needle

I7

Stab/straight stitch (page 73)
Twisted silk thread
Chenille #22 needle

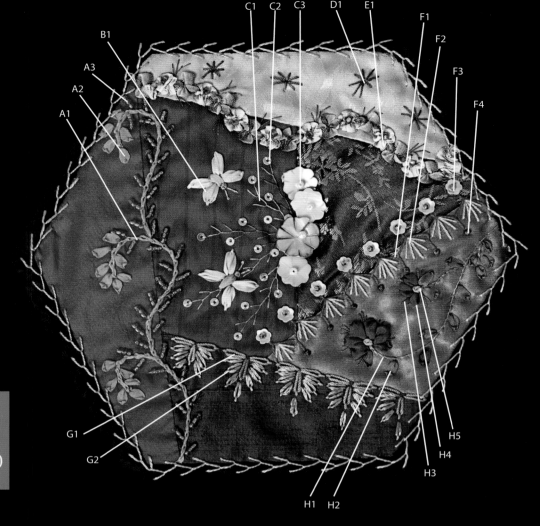

Hexagon 7

(Pattern 7, page 108)

A1
Chain stitch (page 71)
6 strands rayon thread
Chenille #22 needle

A3
Beaded backstitch (page 80)
Nymo thread
Beading needle

C1
Feather stitch (page 72)
1 strand DMC thread
Milliners #7 needle

A2
Ribbon stitch (page 77)
4mm silk ribbon
Chenille #22 needle

B1
Lazy daisy/detached chain
ribbon butterfly (page 87)
4mm silk ribbon
Chenille #22 needle

C2
Sequin fun (page 84)
Nymo thread
Milliners #10 needle

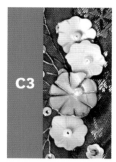

C3

Single-bead button (page 91)
Nymo thread
Milliners #10 needle

F2

Stab/straight stitch (page 73)
Perle cotton #8 thread
Milliners #4 needle

H1

Stem stitch (page 73)
2 strands rayon thread
Milliners #4 needle

F3

Beaded sequin (page 83)
Nymo thread
Milliners #10 needle

H2

Ribbon stitch (page 77)
4mm silk ribbon
Chenille #22 needle

D1

Stab/straight stitch (page 73)
Twisted silk thread
Chenille #22 needle

F4

Colonial knot (page 71)
Perle cotton #8 thread
Milliners #4 needle

H3

Stab/straight stitch (page 73)
Twisted silk thread
Chenille #22 needle

E1

Couched braid or trim (page 90)
Nymo thread
Milliners #10 needle

G1

Lazy daisy / detached chain
stitch (page 72)
Twisted silk thread
Chenille #22 needle

H4

Padded stab stitch (page 77)
7mm silk ribbon
Chenille #22 needle

F1

Cretan stitch (page 72)
Perle cotton #8 thread
Milliners #4 needle

G2

Lazy daisy / detached chain
stitch (page 72)
2 strands rayon thread
Milliners #4 needle

H5

Colonial knot (page 71)
Twisted silk thread
Milliners #4 needle

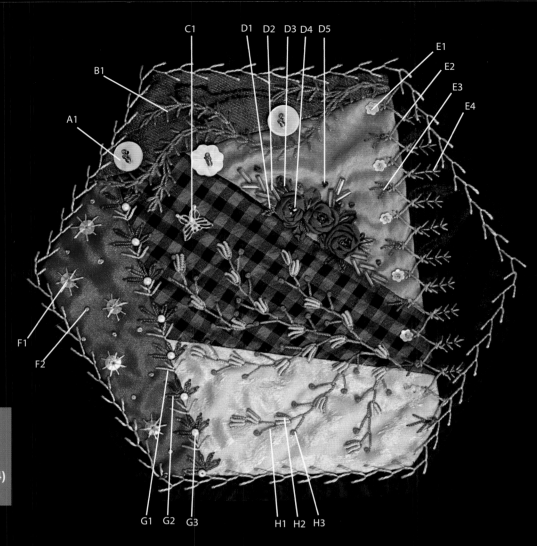

Hexagon 8

(Pattern 3, page 104)

A1

Simple beaded button (page 91)
Nymo thread
Milliners #10 needle

B1

Wheatear stitch (page 73)
Twisted silk thread
Chenille #22 needle

C1

Charm (page 90)
Nymo thread
Milliners #10 needle

D1

Lazy daisy/detached chain
stitch (page 72)
Twisted silk thread
Chenille #22 needle

D2

Bugle bead leaf (page 83)
Nymo thread
Milliners #10 needle

D3

Rosebud (page 88)
4mm silk ribbon and twisted silk thread
Chenille #22 needle

D4

Spider web rose with seed
bead center (page 79)
7mm silk ribbon and Nymo thread
Chenille #22 and milliners #10 needles

E4

Fern stitch (page 72)
1 strand rayon thread
Milliners #7 needle

G3

Single-bead stitch (page 85)
Nymo thread
Milliners #10 needle

D5

Colonial knot (page 71)
Twisted silk thread
Milliners #4 needle

F1

Sequin fun (page 84)
1 strand rayon thread
Milliners #7 needle

H1

Feather stitch (page 72)
Perle cotton #8 thread
Milliners #4 needle

E1

Beaded sequin (page 83)
Nymo thread
Milliners #10 needle

F2

Colonial knot (page 71)
3 strands rayon thread
Milliners #4 needle

H2

Bullion knot (page 70)
Twisted silk thread
Milliners #4 needle

E2

Herringbone stitch (page 72)
Perle cotton #8 thread
Milliners #4 needle

G1

Fly stitch (page 72)
Twisted silk thread
Chenille #22 needle

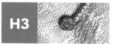

H3

Colonial knot (page 71)
Perle cotton #8 thread
Milliners #4 needle

E3

Stab/straight stitch (page 73)
Twisted silk thread
Milliners #4 needle

G2

Lazy daisy/detached chain
stitch (page 72)
Twisted silk thread
Chenille #22 needle

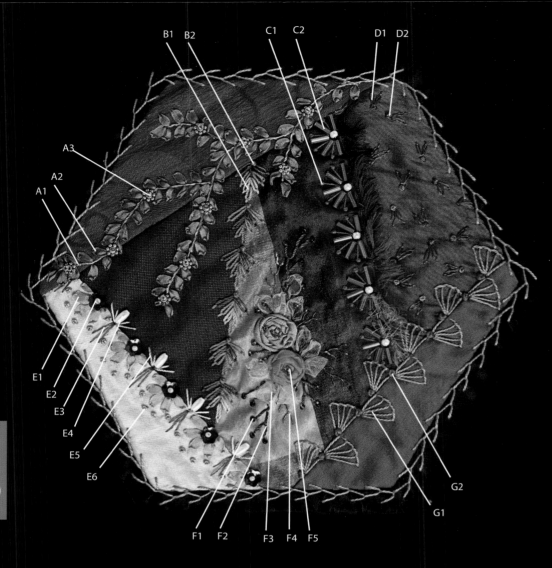

Hexagon 9

(Pattern 3, page 104)

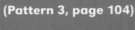

A1
Stem stitch (page 73)
2 strands DMC thread
Milliners #7 needle

A3
Beaded sequin (page 83)
Nymo thread
Milliners #10 needle

B2
Colonial knot (page 71)
Twisted silk thread
Milliners #4 needle

A2
Ribbon stitch (page 77)
4mm silk ribbon
Chenille #22 needle

B1
Lazy daisy / detached chain
stitch (page 72)
Twisted silk thread
Chenille #22 needle

C1
Pistil stitch (page 73)
Perle cotton #12 thread
Milliners #7 needle

C2

Bugle fan (page 84)
Nymo thread
Milliners #10 needle

E4

Single-bead stitch (page 85)
Nymo thread
Milliners #10 needle

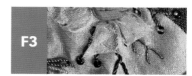

F3

Loop stitch (page 77)
7mm organza ribbon
Chenille #22 needle

D1

Lazy daisy/detached chain
stitch (page 72)
1 strand rayon thread
Milliners #7 needle

E5

Stab/straight stitch (page 73)
Twisted silk thread
Chenille #22 needle

F4

Feather stitch (page 72)
Metallic thread
Chenille #22 needle

D2

Colonial knot (page 71)
Perle cotton #8 thread
Milliners #4 needle

E6

Colonial knot (page 71)
Perle cotton #8 thread
Milliners #4 needle

F5

Spider web rose with seed
bead center (page 79)
7mm silk ribbon and Nymo thread
Chenille #22 and milliners #10 needles

E1

Ribbon stitch (page 77)
4mm silk ribbon
Chenille #22 needle

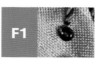

F1

Single-bead stitch (page 85)
Nymo thread
Milliners #10 needle

G1

Buttonhole/blanket stitch fan (page 70)
Perle cotton #8 thread
Milliners #4 needle

E2

Beaded sequin (page 83)
Nymo thread
Milliners #10 needle

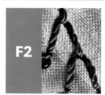

F2

Feather stitch (page 72)
Twisted silk thread
Chenille #22 needle

G2

Colonial knot (page 71)
Perle cotton #8 thread
Milliners #4 needle

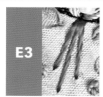

E3

Stab/straight stitch (page 73)
1 strand rayon thread
Milliners #7 needle

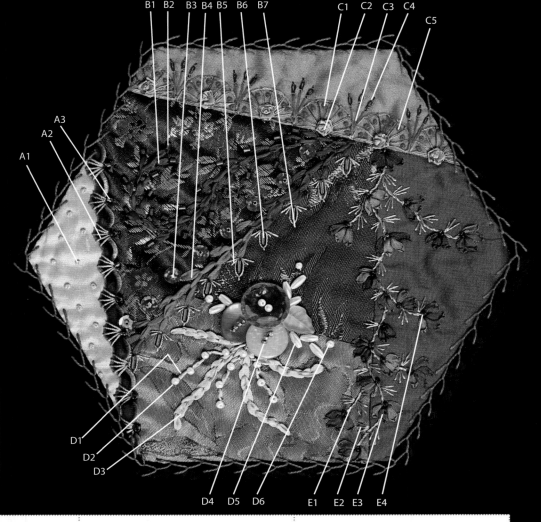

Hexagon 10

(Pattern 9, page 110)

A1

Colonial knot (page 71)
Perle cotton #8 thread
Milliners #7 needle

B1

Feather stitch (page 72)
4mm silk ribbon
Chenille #22 needle

B4

Feather stitch (page 72)
4mm silk ribbon
Chenille #22 needle

A2

Couched rickrack (page 90)
Perle cotton #8 thread
Milliners #4 needle

B2

Single-bead stitch (page 85)
Nymo thread
Milliners #10 needle

B5

Stab/straight stitch (page 73)
Perle cotton #12 thread
Milliners #7 needle

A3

Single-bead stitch (page 85)
Nymo thread
Milliners #10 needle

B3

Beaded sequin (page 83)
Nymo thread
Milliners #10 needle

B6

Single-bead stitch (page 85)
Nymo thread
Milliners #10 needle

B7

Lazy daisy/detached chain
stitch (page 72)
Perle cotton #12 thread
Milliners #7 needle

D1

Twisted stab stitch (page 79)
4mm silk ribbon
Chenille #22 needle

D5

Bugle bead leaf (page 83)
Nymo thread
Milliners #10 needle

C1

Buttonhole/blanket stitch fan (page 70)
2 strands DMC thread
Milliners #7 needle

D2

Single-bead stitch (page 85)
Nymo thread
Milliners #10 needle

D6

Single-bead stitch (page 85)
Nymo thread
Milliners #10 needle

C2

Ruched rose (page 78)
4mm silk ribbon
Chenille #22 needle

D3

Split stitch (page 79)
4mm silk ribbon
Chenille #22 needle

E1

Stem stitch (page 73)
2 strands rayon thread
Milliners #4 needle

C3

Stab/straight stitch (page 73)
2 strands DMC thread
Milliners #7 needle

E2

Stab/straight stitch page 73)
1 strand rayon thread
Milliners #7 needle

C4

Lazy daisy/detached chain
stitch (page 72)
1 strand rayon thread
Milliners #7 needle

D4

Button cluster (page 90)
Nymo thread
Milliners #10 needle

E3

Ribbon stitch (page 77)
4mm silk ribbon
Chenille #22 needle

E4

Single-bead stitch (page 85)
Nymo thread
Milliners #10 needle

C5

Colonial knot (page 71)
Perle cotton #12 thread
Milliners #7 needle

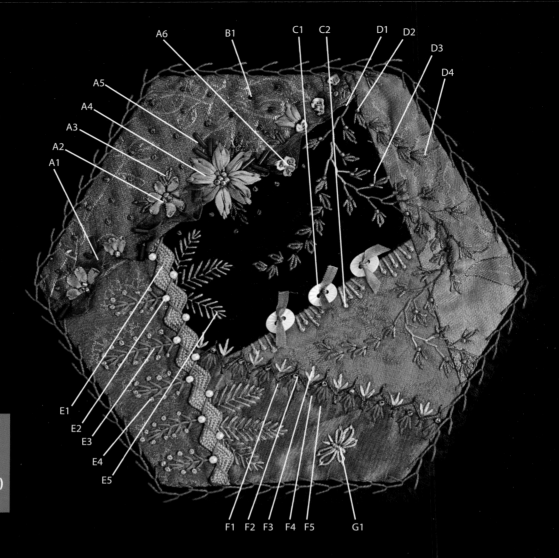

Hexagon 11

(Pattern 7, page 108)

A1

Couched ribbon garland (page 90)
Nymo thread
Milliners #10 needle

A3

Lazy daisy/detached chain
stitch (page 72)
Twisted silk thread
Chenille #22 needle

A5

Bugle bead leaf (page 83)
Nymo thread
Milliners #10 needle

A2

Ribbon stitch flower with colonial knot center (page 77)
4mm silk ribbon and perle
cotton #8 thread
Chenille #22 and milliners #4 needles

A4

Lazy daisy/detached chain stitch flower
with seed bead center (page 76)
7mm silk ribbon and Nymo thread
Chenille #22 and milliners #10 needles

A6

Loop stitch with colonial knot (page 76)
4mm silk ribbon and twisted silk thread
Chenille #22 needle

B1

Colonial knot (page 71)
Twisted silk thread
Milliners #4 needle

C1

Tied button (page 91)
4mm silk ribbon
Chenille #22 needle

E1

Couched rickrack (page 90)
Perle cotton #8 thread
Milliners #4 needle

F2

Single-bead stitch (page 85)
Nymo thread
Milliners #10 needle

C2

Pistil stitch (page 73)
Perle cotton #8 thread
Milliners #4 needle

E2

Single-bead stitch (page 85)
Nymo thread
Milliners #10 needle

F3

Stab/straight stitch (page 73)
2 strands rayon thread
Milliners #4 needle

D1

Feather stitch (page 72)
Twisted silk thread
Chenille #22 needle

E3

Fly stitch (page 72)
Perle cotton #8 thread
Milliners #4 needle

F4

Stab/straight stitch (page 73)
Perle cotton #8 thread
Milliners #4 needle

D2

Single-bead stitch (page 85)
Nymo thread
Milliners #10 needle

E4

Colonial knot (page 71)
Perle cotton #8 thread
Milliners #4 needle

F5

Lazy daisy/detached chain
stitch (page 72)
Perle cotton #8 thread
Milliners #7 needle

D3

Stab/straight stitch (page 73)
Twisted silk thread
Chenille #22 needle

E5

Fly stitch leaf (page 72)
2 strands DMC thread
Milliners #7 needle

G1

Lazy daisy/detached chain
stitch butterfly (page 87)
Twisted silk thread
Milliners #4 needle

D4

Lazy daisy/detached chain
stitch (page 72)
Twisted silk thread
Chenille #22 needle

F1

Cretan stitch (page 72)
Twisted silk thread
Chenille #22 needle

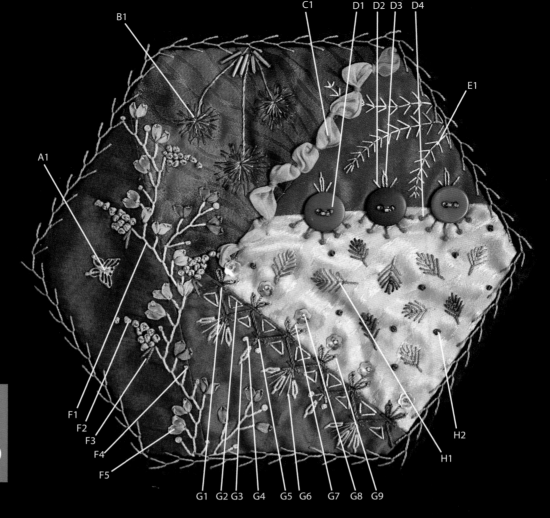

Hexagon 12

(Pattern 4, page 105)

A1

Charm (page 90)
Nymo thread
Milliners #10 needle

B1

Agapanthus (page 86)
1 strand rayon thread
Milliners #7 needle

C1

Stab-stitch couching (page 91)
11mm silk ribbon and 4mm silk ribbon
Chenille #22 needle

D1

Simple beaded button (page 91)
Nymo thread
Milliners #10 needle

D2

Stab/straight stitch (page 73)
Perle cotton #12 thread
Milliners #7 needle

D3

Lazy daisy / detached chain
stitch (page 72)
Perle cotton #12 thread
Milliners #7 needle

D4

Pistil stitch (page 73)
Perle cotton #12 thread
Milliners #7 needle

E1

Fern stitch (page 72)
Perle cotton #12 thread
Milliners #7 needle

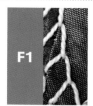

F1

Feather stitch (page 72)
Perle cotton #8 thread
Milliners #4 needle

G2

Stab/straight stitch (page 73)
Perle cotton #12 thread
Milliners #7 needle

G7

Stab/straight stitch (page 73)
Twisted silk thread
Chenille #22 needle

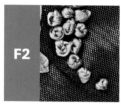

F2

Colonial knot (page 71)
4mm silk ribbon
Chenille #22 needle

G3

Lazy daisy/detached chain
stitch (page 72)
Twisted silk thread
Chenille #22 needle

G8

Beaded sequin (page 83)
Nymo thread
Milliners #10 needle

F3

Stab/straight stitch (page 73)
Twisted silk thread
Milliners #7 needle

G4

Colonial knot (page 71)
Perle cotton #8 thread
Milliners #4 needle

G9

Lazy daisy/detached chain
stitch (page 72)
Twisted silk thread
Chenille #22 needle

F4

Colonial knot (page 71)
Perle cotton #8 thread
Milliners #7 needle

G5

Stab/straight stitch (page 73)
Twisted silk thread
Chenille #22 needle

H1

Fly stitch leaf (page 72)
Twisted silk thread
Chenille #22 needle

F5

Ribbon stitch (page 77)
4mm silk ribbon
Chenille #22 needle

G6

Stab/straight stitch (page 73)
Perle cotton #12 thread
Milliners #7 needle

H2

Colonial knot (page 71)
Perle cotton #8 thread
Milliners #7 needle

G1

Chevron stitch (page 71)
Twisted silk thread
Chenille #22 needle

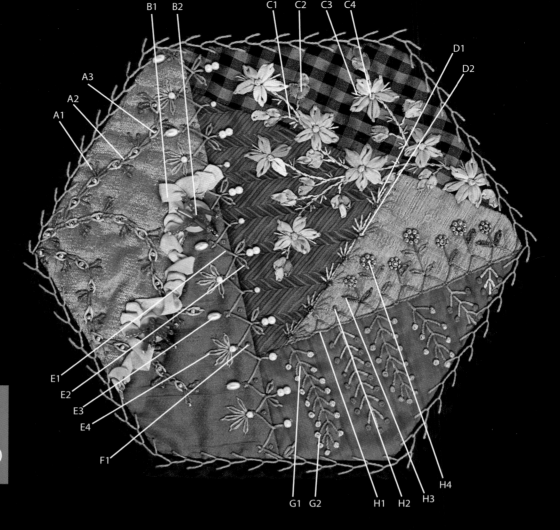

Hexagon 13

(Pattern 6, page 107)

A1
Pistil stitch (page 73)
Perle cotton #12 thread
Milliners #7 needle

A2
Alternating chain stitch (page 70)
Perle cotton #12 thread
Milliners #7 needle

A3
Single-bead stitch (page 85)
Nymo thread
Milliners #10 needle

B1
Plume stitch (page 77)
7mm silk ribbon
Chenille #22 needle

B2
Simple beaded button (page 91),
upright bugle beads and
beaded tassel (page 85)
Nymo thread
Beading needle

C1
Stem stitch (page 73)
Perle cotton #12 thread
Milliners #7 needle

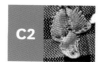

C2

Ribbon stitch (page 77)
4mm silk ribbon
Chenille #22 needle

E2

Lazy daisy/detached chain
stitch (page 72)
Perle cotton #8 thread
Milliners #4 needle

G2

Colonial knot (page 71)
Perle cotton #8 thread
Milliners #4 needle

C3

Stab/straight stitch (page 73)
Perle cotton #12 thread
Milliners #7 needle

E3

Single-bead stitch (page 85)
Nymo thread
Milliners #10 needle

H1

Closed buttonhole/blanket
stitch (page 71)
Perle cotton #12 thread
Milliners #7 needle

C4

Lazy daisy/detached chain stitch flower
with colonial knot center (page 76)
4mm silk ribbon
Chenille #22 needle

E4

Lazy daisy/detached chain
stitch (page 72)
1 strand rayon thread
Milliners #7 needle

H2

Colonial knot (page 71)
Perle cotton #12 thread
Milliners #7 needle

D1

Stab/straight stitch (page 73)
Twisted silk and twisted rayon thread
Chenille #22 needle

F1

Colonial knot (page 71)
Perle cotton #12 thread
Milliners #7 needle

H3

Lazy daisy/detached chain
stitch (page 72)
Twisted silk thread
Chenille #22 needle

D2

Single-bead stitch (page 85)
Nymo thread
Milliners #10 needle

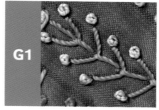

G1

Fly stitch (page 72)
Perle cotton #8 thread
Milliners #4 needle

H4

Beaded sequin (page 83)
Nymo thread
Milliners #10 needle

E1

Cretan and herringbone stitch
combination (page 71)
Perle cotton #8 thread
Milliners #4 needle

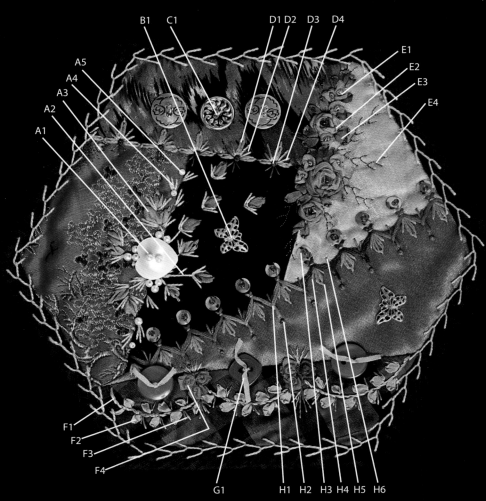

B1 C1   D1 D2 D3 D4
                                    E1
A5   E2
A4   E3
A3   E4
A2
A1

Hexagon 14

(Pattern 5, page 106)

F1
F2
F3
F4

G1   H1 H2 H3 H4 H5 H6

A1

Simple beaded button (page 91)
Nymo thread
Milliners #10 needle

A4

Stab/straight stitch (page 73)
Perle cotton #8 thread
Milliners #4 needle

C1

Simple beaded button (page 91)
Nymo thread
Milliners #10 needle

A2

Fly stitch (page 72)
Perle cotton #8 thread
Milliners #4 needle

A5

Single-bead stitch (page 85)
Nymo thread
Milliners #10 needle

D1

Lazy daisy / detached chain
stitch (page 72)
2 strands rayon thread
Milliners #7 needle

A3

Rosebud (page 88)
4mm silk ribbon and perle
cotton #8 thread
Chenille #22 and milliners #4 needles

B1

Charm (page 90)
Nymo thread
Milliners #10 needle

D2

Stab/straight stitch (page 73)
Twisted silk thread
Chenille #22 needle

D3
Colonial knot (page 71)
Perle cotton #8 thread
Milliners #4 needle

F2
Ribbon stitch (page 77)
4mm silk ribbon
Chenille #22 needle

H2
Colonial knot (page 71)
Perle cotton #12 thread
Milliners #7 needle

D4
Stab/straight stitch (page 73)
1 strand rayon thread
Milliners #7 needle

F3
Stab/straight stitch (page 73)
1 strand rayon thread
Milliners #7 needle

H3
Beaded sequin (page 83)
Nymo thread
Milliners #10 needle

E1
Loop stitch with colonial knot (page 76)
7mm silk ribbon and Nymo thread
Chenille #22 and milliners #10 needles

F4
Ruched rose (page 78)
4mm silk ribbon
Chenille #22 needle

H4
Stab/straight stitch (page 73)
2 strands rayon thread
Milliners #7 needle

E2
Spider web rose with beaded
center (page 79)
7mm silk ribbon and Nymo thread
Chenille #22 and milliners #10 needles

G1
Tied button (page 91)
2mm silk ribbon
Chenille #22 needle

H5
Lazy daisy / detached chain
stitch (page 72)
2 strands rayon thread
Milliners #7 needle

E3
Ribbon stitch (page 77)
4mm silk ribbon
Chenille #22 needle

H6
Stab/straight stitch (page 73)
1 strand DMC thread
Milliners #7 needle

E4
Feather stitch (page 72)
Metallic thread
Chenille #22 needle

H1
Cretan stitch (page 72)
6 strands DMC thread
Chenille #22 needle

F1
Stem stitch (page 73)
3 strands rayon thread
Milliners #4 needle

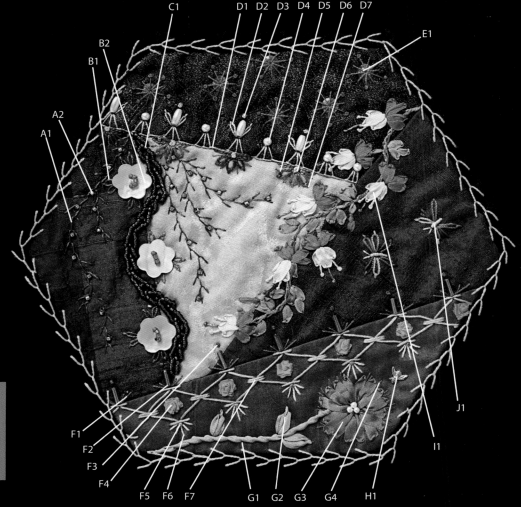

C1   D1 D2 D3 D4 D5 D6 D7

B2

B1

E1

A2

A1

Hexagon 15

(Pattern 1, page 102)

F1
F2
F3
F4
F5   F6   F7   G1 G2 G3   G4   H1

J1

I1

A1

Feather stitch (page 72)
1 strand rayon thread
Milliners #7 needle

A2

Single-bead stitch (page 85)
Nymo thread
Milliners #10 needle

B1

Lazy daisy / detached chain
stitch (page 72)
Perle cotton #12 thread
Milliners #7 needle

B2

Simple beaded button (page 91)
Nymo thread
Milliners #10 needle

C1

Beaded chain (page 81)
Nymo thread
Milliners #10 needle

D1

Closed buttonhole/blanket
stitch (page 71)
Perle cotton #12 thread
Milliners #7 needle

D2

Lazy daisy / detached chain
stitch (page 72)
Perle cotton #12 thread
Milliners #7 needle

D3

Colonial knot (page 71)
Perle cotton #12 thread
Milliners #7 needle

D4

Single-bead stitch (page 85)
Nymo thread
Milliners #10 needle

F3

Colonial knot (page 71)
Perle cotton #12 thread
Milliners #7 needle

G3

Ribbon stitch flower with
beaded center (page 77)
4mm silk ribbon and Nymo thread
Chenille #22 and milliners #10 needles

D5

Stab/straight stitch (page 73)
1 strand rayon thread
Milliners #7 needle

F4

Ruched rose (page 78)
4mm silk ribbon
Chenille #22 needle

D6

Colonial knot (page 71)
Perle cotton #8 thread
Milliners #4 needle

F5

Single-bead stitch (page 85)
Nymo thread
Milliners #10 needle

G4

Stab/straight stitch (page 73)
Perle cotton #12
Milliners #7 needle

D7

Lazy daisy/detached chain
stitch (page 72)
Perle cotton #8 thread
Milliners #4 needle

F6

Stab/straight stitch (page 73)
Perle cotton #12 thread
Milliners #7 needle

H1

Charm (page 90)
Nymo thread
Milliners #10 needle

E1

Sequin fun (page 84)
Perle cotton #12 thread
Milliners #7 needle

F7

Chevron stitch (page 71)
Perle cotton #8 thread
Milliners #4 needle

I1

Fuchsia (page 86)
4mm silk ribbon and perle
cotton #12 thread
Chenille #22 and milliners #7 needles

F1

Stab/straight stitch (page 73)
Perle cotton #12 thread
Milliners #7 needle

G1

Whipped chain stitch (page 79)
4mm silk ribbon and perle
cotton #12 thread
Chenille #22 and milliners #7 needles

F2

Single-bead stitch (page 85)
Nymo thread
Milliners #10 needle

G2

Lazy daisy/detached chain
stitch—silk ribbon (page 76)
4mm silk ribbon
Chenille #22 needle

J1

Lazy daisy/detached chain
butterfly (page 87)
Twisted silk thread
Chenille #22 needle

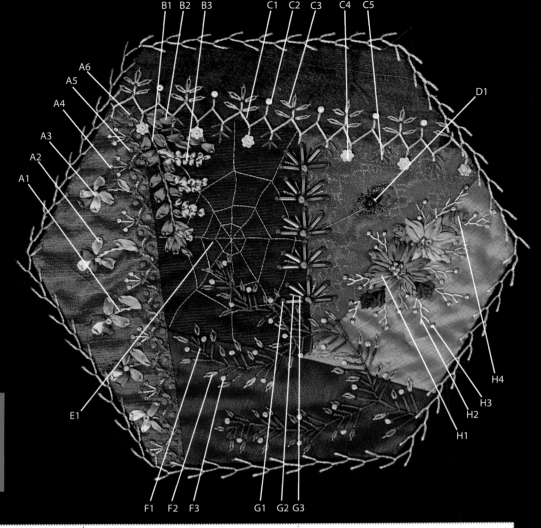

B1 B2 B3   C1 C2 C3   C4 C5

A6
A5
A4
A3
A2
A1

D1

E1

H4
H3
H2
H1

F1 F2 F3   G1 G2 G3

Hexagon 16

(Pattern 7, page 108)

A1

Stem stitch (page 73)
Perle cotton #12 thread
Milliners #7 needle

A2

Ribbon stitch flower with
beaded center (page 77)
4mm silk ribbon and Nymo thread
Chenille #22 and milliners #10 needles

A3

Single-bead stitch (page 85)
Nymo thread
Milliners #10 needle

A4

Pistil stitch (page 73)
Perle cotton #12 thread
Milliners #7 needle

A5

Colonial knot (page 71)
Perle cotton #12 thread
Milliners #7 needle

A6

Whipped herringbone stitch (page 73)
Perle cotton #8 thread
Milliners #4 needle

B1

Stem stitch (page 73)
2 strands DMC thread
Milliners #7 needle

B2

Ribbon stitch (page 77)
4mm silk ribbon
Chenille #22 needle

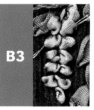

B3

Stab stitch—silk ribbon (page 79)
4mm silk ribbon
Chenille #22 needle

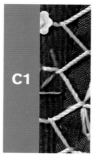

C1

Cretan stitch (page 72)
Twisted silk thread
Chenille #22 needle

E1

Round spider web (page 88)
Metallic thread
Chenille #22 needle

G3

Bugle fan (page 84)
Nymo thread
Milliners #10 needle

H1

Lazy daisy/detached chain stitch flower
with seed bead center (page 76)
7mm silk ribbon and Nymo thread
Chenille #22 and milliners #10 needles

C2

Single-bead stitch (page 85)
Nymo thread
Milliners #10 needle

F1

Fly stitch (page 72)
Twisted silk thread
Chenille #22 needle

C3

Lazy daisy/detached chain
stitch (page 72)
1 strand rayon thread
Milliners #7 needle

F2

Lazy daisy/detached chain
stitch (page 72)
2 strands DMC thread
Milliners #7 needle

H2

Feather stitch (page 72)
Perle cotton #12 thread
Milliners #7 needle

C4

Beaded sequin (page 83)
Nymo thread
Milliners #10 needle

F3

Colonial knot (page 71)
Perle cotton #12 thread
Milliners #7 needle

H3

Single-bead stitch (page 85)
Nymo thread
Milliners #10 needle

C5

Stab/straight stitch (page 73)
Perle cotton #12 thread
Milliners #7 needle

G1

Colonial knot (page 71)
Perle cotton #12 thread
Milliners #7 needle

H4

Fishbone stitch leaf (page 76)
4mm silk ribbon
Chenille #22 needle

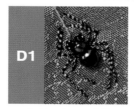

D1

Spider (page 89)
Metallic and Nymo thread
Milliners #10 and chenille #22 needles

G2

Stab/straight stitch (page 73)
Perle cotton #12 thread
Milliners #7 needle

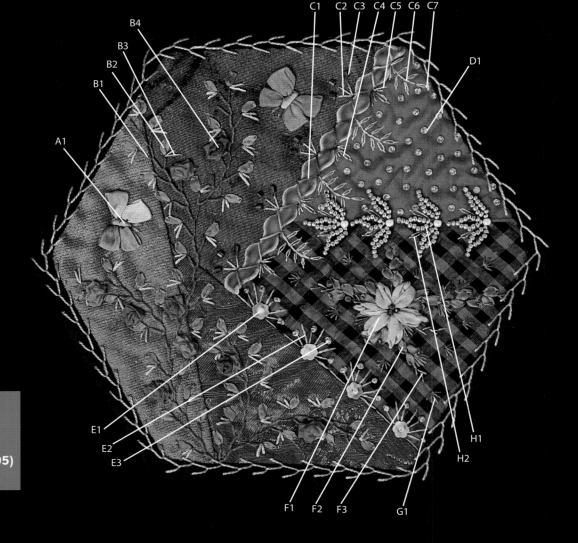

Hexagon 17

(Pattern 4, page 105)

A1

Loop stitch butterfly (page 87)
7mm silk ribbon
Chenille #22 needle

B2

Ribbon stitch (page 77)
4mm silk ribbon
Chenille #22 needle

B4

Ruched rose (page 78)
4mm silk ribbon
Chenille #22 needle

B1

Feather stitch (page 72)
Perle cotton #8 thread
Milliners #4 needle

B3

Stab/straight stitch (page 73)
Twisted silk thread
Chenille #22 needle

C1

Couched rickrack (page 90)
Twisted silk thread
Chenille #22 needle

C2

Stab/straight stitch (page 73)
Perle cotton #12 thread
Milliners #7 needle

D1

Beaded sequin (page 83)
Nymo thread
Milliners #10 needle

F2

Ribbon stitch (page 77)
4mm silk ribbon
Chenille #22 needle

C3

Single-bead stitch (page 85)
Nymo thread
Milliners #10 needle

E1

Beaded sequin (page 83)
Nymo thread
Milliners #10 needle

F3

Stab/straight stitch (page 73)
1 strand rayon thread
Milliners #7 needle

C4

Lazy daisy/detached chain
stitch (page 72)
1 strand rayon thread
Milliners #7 needle

E2

Stab/straight stitch (page 73)
1 strand rayon thread
Milliners #7 needle

G1

Stab/straight stitch (page 73)
1 strand rayon thread
Milliners #7 needle

C5

Stab/straight stitch (page 73)
1 strand rayon thread
Milliners #7 needle

E3

Colonial knot (page 71)
Perle cotton #8 thread
Milliners #4 needle

H1

Beaded pointed petal (page 82)
Nymo thread
Beading needle

C6

Stem stitch (page 73)
1 strand DMC thread
Milliners #7 needle

H2

Lazy daisy/detached chain
stitch (page 72)
Perle cotton #12 thread
Milliners #7 needle

F1

Lazy daisy/detached chain stitch
flower with beaded center (page 76)
7mm silk ribbon and Nymo thread
Chenille #22 and milliners #10 needles

C7

Lazy daisy/detached chain
stitch (page 72)
1 strand DMC thread
Milliners #7 needle

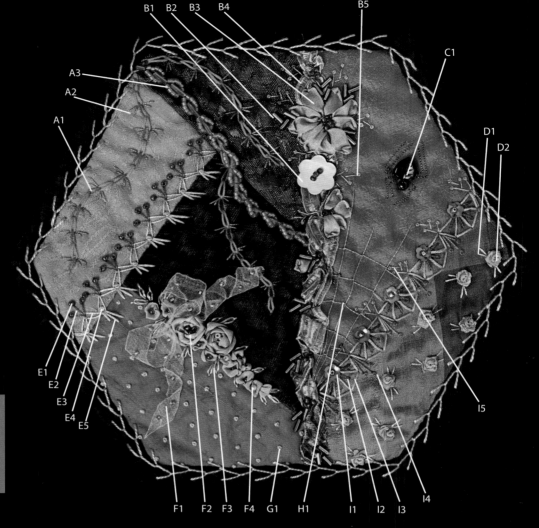

Hexagon 18

(Pattern 5, page 106)

A1

Alternating chain stitch (page 70)
Perle cotton #12 thread
Milliners #7 needle

A2

Stab/straight stitch (page 73)
Perle cotton #12 thread
Milliners #7 needle

A3

Bugle and seed bead chain (page 84)
Nymo thread
Beading needle

B1

Simple beaded button (page 91)
Nymo thread
Milliners #10 needle

B2

Bugle bead leaf (page 83)
Nymo thread
Milliners #10 needle

B3

Ribbon stitch flower with
beaded center (page 77)
7mm silk ribbon and Nymo thread
Chenille #22 and milliners #10 needles

B4

Couched ribbon garland (page 90)
Nymo thread
Milliners #10 needle

B5

Pistil stitch (page 73)
1 strand DMC thread
Milliners #7 needle

E4

Colonial knot (page 71)
Perle cotton #8 thread
Milliners #4 needle

G1

Colonial knot (page 71)
Perle cotton #8 thread
Milliners #4 needle

C1

Spider (page 89)
Nymo thread
Milliners #10 needle

E5

Stab/straight stitch (page 73)
Perle cotton #8 thread
Milliners #4 needle

H1

Straight spider web (page 89)
Metallic thread
Chenille #22 needle

D1

Stab/straight stitch (page 73)
Perle cotton #12 thread
Milliners #7 needle

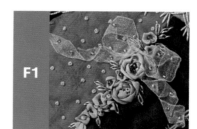

F1

Couched ribbon garland (page 90)
Nymo thread
Milliners #10 needle

I1

Beaded sequin (page 83)
Nymo thread
Milliners #10 needle

I2

Stab/straight stitch (page 73)
Twisted silk thread
Chenille #22 needle

D2

Ruched rose (page 78)
4mm silk ribbon
Chenille #22 needle

E1

Single-bead stitch (page 85)
Nymo thread
Beading #10 needle

F2

Spider web rose with seed
bead center (page 79)
7mm silk ribbon and Nymo thread
Chenille #22 and milliners #10 needles

I3

Buttonhole/blanket stitch fan (page 70)
Perle cotton #8 thread
Milliners #4 needle

E2

Stab/straight stitch (page 73)
Perle cotton #12 thread
Milliners #7 needle

F3

Lazy daisy/detached chain
stitch (page 72)
1 strand rayon thread
Milliners #7 needle

I4

Pistil stitch (page 73)
Perle cotton #12 thread
Milliners #7 needle

E3

Zigzag chain stitch (page 74)
Perle cotton #12 thread
Milliners #7 needle

F4

Loop stitch with bead (page 76)
7mm silk ribbon and Nymo thread
Chenille #22 and milliners #10 needles

I5

Pistil stitch (page 73)
1 strand DMC thread
Milliners #7 needle

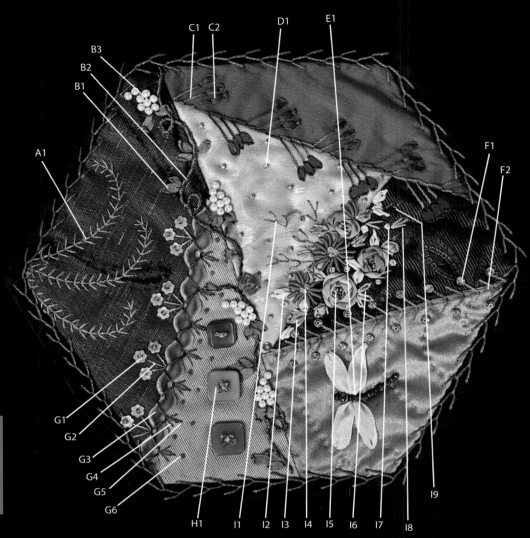

Hexagon 19

(Pattern 6, page 107)

A1

Fern stitch (page 72)
1 strand rayon thread
Milliners #7 needle

B1

Ribbon stitch (page 77)
4mm silk ribbon
Milliners #22 needle

B2

Stem stitch (page 73)
Stranded silk thread
Chenille #22 needle

B3

Beaded grapes (page 82)
Nymo thread
Milliners #10 needle

C1

Straight feather stitch (page 73)
Twisted silk thread
Chenille #22 needle

C2

Ribbon stitch (page 77)
4mm silk ribbon
Chenille #22 needle

D1

Single-bead stitch (page 85)
Nymo thread
Milliners #10 needle

G4

Stab/straight stitch (page 73)
1 strand rayon thread
Milliners #7 needle

I4

Bullion knot flower with
colonial knot center (page 70)
Twisted silk thread
Milliners #7 needle

E1

Dragonfly (page 86)
7mm silk ribbon and Nymo thread
Chenille #22 and beading needles

G5

Lazy daisy/detached chain
stitch (page 72)
1 strand rayon thread
Milliners #7 needle

I5

Spider web rose with seed
bead center (page 79)
7mm silk ribbon and Nymo thread
Chenille #22 and milliners #10 needles

F1

Beaded sequin (page 83)
Nymo thread
Milliners #10 needle

G6

Colonial knot (page 71)
Perle cotton #12 thread
Milliners #7 needle

I6

Lazy daisy/detached chain
stitch (page 72)
2 strands rayon thread
Milliners #4 needle

F2

Wheatear stitch (page 73)
Twisted silk thread
Chenille #22 needle

H1

Simple beaded button (page 91)
Nymo thread
Milliners #10 needle

I7

Colonial knot (page 71)
4mm silk ribbon
Chenille #22 needle

G1

Beaded sequin (page 83)
Nymo thread
Milliners #10 needle

I1

Feather stitch (page 72)
1 strand rayon thread
Milliners #7 needle

I8

Stab/straight stitch (page 73)
Twisted silk thread
Chenille #22 needle

G2

Stab/straight stitch (page 73)
1 strand rayon thread
Milliners #10 needle

I2

Lazy daisy/detached chain
stitch—silk ribbon (page 76)
4mm silk ribbon
Chenille #22 needle

I9

Stab/straight stitch (page 73)
1 strand rayon thread
Milliners #7 needle

G3

Couched rickrack (page 90)
Twisted silk thread
Chenille #22 needle

I3

Rosebud (page 88)
4mm silk ribbon and
2 strands rayon thread
Chenille #22 and milliners #4 needles

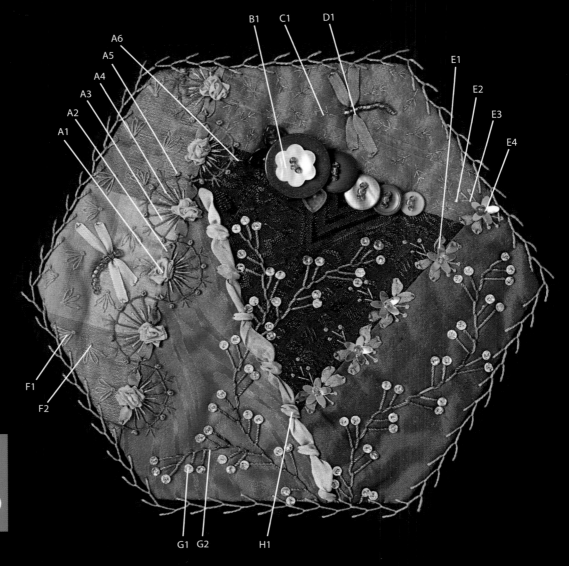

Hexagon 20

(Pattern 1, page 102)

A1
Ruched rose (page 78)
7mm silk ribbon
Chenille #22 needle

A3
Buttonhole/blanket stitch fan (page 70)
Perle cotton #12 thread
Milliners #7 needle

A5
Colonial knot (page 71)
Perle cotton #12 thread
Milliners #7 needle

A2
Ribbon stitch (page 77)
4mm silk ribbon
Chenille #22 needle

A4
Stab/straight stitch (page 73)
2 strands DMC thread
Milliners #7 needle

A6
Stab/straight stitch (page 73)
1 strand DMC thread
Milliners #7 needle

B1

Layered buttons (page 91) and
button cluster (page 90)
Nymo thread
Milliners #10 needle

C1

Fern stitch (page 72)
Metallic thread
Chenille #22 needle

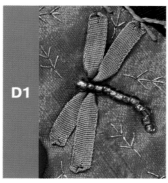

D1

Dragonfly (page 86)
4mm silk ribbon and Nymo thread
Chenille #22 and beading needles

E1

Ribbon stitch (page 77)
4mm silk ribbon
Chenille #22 needle

E2

Colonial knot (page 71)
2 strands DMC thread
Milliners #7 needle

E3

Stab/straight stitch (page 73)
1 strand DMC thread
Milliners #7 needle

E4

Beaded sequin (page 83)
Nymo thread
Milliners #10 needle

F1

Lazy daisy/detached chain
stitch (page 72)
1 strand DMC thread
Milliners #7 needle

F2

Colonial knot (page 71)
2 strands DMC thread
Milliners #7 needle

G1

Beaded sequin (page 83)
Nymo thread
Milliners #10 needle

G2

Straight feather stitch (page 73)
Twisted rayon thread
Chenille #22 needle

H1

Coral stitch (page 76)
7mm silk ribbon
Chenille #22 needle

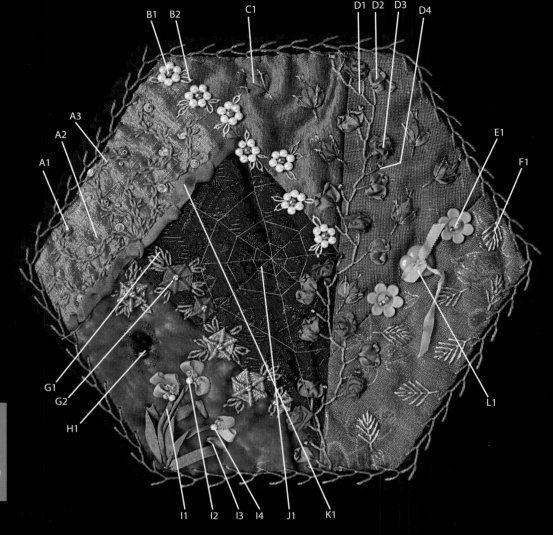

Hexagon 21

(Pattern 5, page 106)

A1

Beaded sequin (page 83)
Nymo thread
Milliners #10 needle

A2

Stab/straight stitch (page 73)
Perle cotton #8 thread
Milliners #4 needle

A3

Chain stitch (page 71)
Perle cotton #8 thread
Milliners #4 needle

B1

Beaded forget-me-not (page 82)
Nymo thread
Milliners #10 needle

B2

Lazy daisy/detached chain
stitch (page 72)
Perle cotton #8 thread
Milliners #4 needle

C1

Rosebud (page 88)
4mm silk ribbon and
1 strand rayon thread
Chenille #22 and milliners #7 needles

Feather stitch (page 72)
Perle cotton #8 thread
Milliners #4 needle

Lazy daisy/detached chain
stitch (page 72)
Perle cotton #8 thread
Milliners #4 needle

Bent stab stitch (page 75)
4mm silk ribbon and
1 strand DMC thread
Chenille #22 and milliners #7 needles

Ribbon stitch (page 77)
4mm silk ribbon
Chenille #22 needle

Woven spider web (page 74)
Perle cotton #8 thread
Milliners #4 needle

Single Bead Stitch (page 85)
Nymo thread
Milliners #10 needle

Ruched rose (page 78)
7mm silk ribbon
Chenille #22 needle

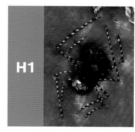

Spider (page 89)
Nymo and metallic thread
Chenille #22 and milliners #10 needles

Round spider web (page 88)
Metallic thread
Chenille #22 needle

Single-bead stitch (page 85)
Nymo thread
Milliners #10 needle

Simple beaded button (page 91)
4mm silk ribbon and Nymo thread
Chenille #22 and milliners #10 needles

Twisted stab stitch (page 79)
4mm silk ribbon
Chenille #22 needle

Coral stitch (page 76)
7mm silk ribbon
Chenille #22 needle

Fly stitch leaf (page 72)
Twisted rayon thread
Chenille #22 needle

Loop stitch and flower (page 77)
4mm silk ribbon
Chenille #22 needle

Bow button (page 90)
4mm silk ribbon
Chenille #22 needle

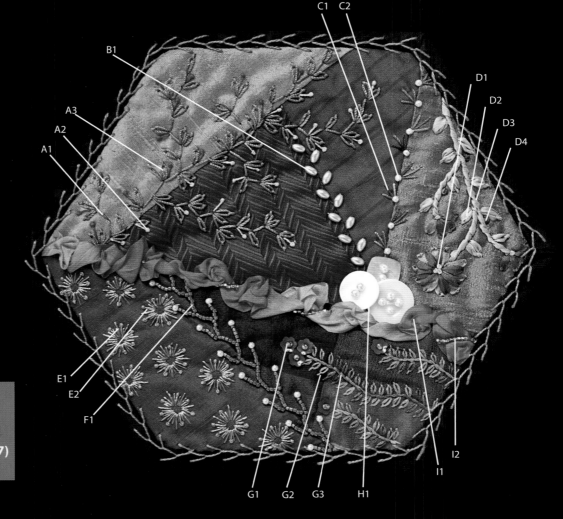

C1 C2
B1
A3
A2
A1
D1
D2
D3
D4

E1
E2
F1

Hexagon 22

(Pattern 6, page 107)

G1 G2 G3 H1

I1
I2

A1

Stab/straight stitch (page 73)
Twisted rayon thread
Chenille #22 needle

A3

Lazy daisy / detached chain
stitch (page 72)
Twisted rayon thread
Chenille #22 needle

C1

Stab/straight stitch (page 73)
Twisted silk thread
Milliners #22 needle

A2

Pistil stitch (page 73)
Perle cotton #12 thread
Milliners #7 needle

B1

Single-bead stitch (page 85)
Nymo thread
Milliners #10 needle

C2

Single-bead stitch (page 85)
Nymo thread
Milliners #10 needle

E1

Stab/straight stitch (page 73)
1 strand rayon thread
Milliners #7 needle

G3

Stem stitch (page 73)
2 strands DMC thread
Milliners #7 needle

D1

Ribbon stitch flower with colonial knot center (page 77)
4mm silk ribbon and perle cotton #8 thread
Chenille #22 and milliners #4 needles

E2

Pistil stitch (page 73)
Perle cotton #12 thread
Milliners #7 needle

H1

Simple beaded button (page 91)
Nymo thread
Milliners #10 needle

D2

Lazy daisy/detached chain stitch—silk ribbon (page 76)
4mm silk ribbon
Chenille #22 needle

F1

Beaded feather stitch (page 81)
Nymo thread
Beading needle

I1

Ruched silk ribbon garland (page 78)
11mm silk ribbon and Nymo thread
Milliners #10 needle

D3

Whipped chain stitch (page 79)
4mm silk ribbon and perle cotton #12 thread
Chenille #22 and milliners #7 needles

G1

Beaded sequin (page 83)
Nymo thread
Milliners #10 needle

I2

String of beads (page 85)
Nymo thread
Beading needle

D4

Colonial knot (page 71)
4mm silk ribbon
Chenille #22 needle

G2

Lazy daisy/detached chain stitch (page 72)
2 strands DMC thread
Milliners #7 needle

Hexagon 23

(Pattern 8, page 109)

A1

Delphinium (page 86)
4mm and 7mm silk ribbon and
perle cotton #12 thread
Chenille #22 and milliners #7 needles

B1

Straight feather stitch (page 73)
Perle cotton #8 thread
Milliners #4 needle

B2

Stab/straight stitch (page 73)
Perle cotton #12 thread
Milliners #7 needle

B3

Colonial knot (page 71)
Perle cotton #8 thread
Milliners #4 needle

B4

Beaded sequin (page 83)
Nymo thread
Milliners #10 needle

B5

Lazy daisy/detached chain
stitch (page 72)
Perle cotton #12 thread
Milliners #7 needle

E4

Whipped chain stitch (page 79)
3 strands rayon thread
Milliners #4 needle

G3

Lazy daisy/detached chain
stitch (page 72)
Twisted silk thread
Chenille #22 needle

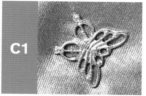

C1

Charm (page 90)
Nymo thread
Milliners #10 needle

F1

Knotted couched ribbon (page 91)
7mm silk ribbon and Nymo thread
Milliners #10 needle

G4

Colonial knot (page 71)
3 strands rayon thread
Milliners #4 needle

D1

Single-bead stitch (page 85)
Nymo thread
Milliners #10 needle

F2

Stab/straight stitch (page 73)
1 strand rayon thread
Milliners #7 needle

H1

Rosebud (page 88)
4mm silk ribbon and twisted silk thread
Chenille #22 needle

D2

Stab/straight stitch (page 73)
Twisted silk thread
Chenille #22 needle

F3

Simple beaded button (page 91)
Nymo thread
Milliners #10 needle

H2

Colonial knot (page 71)
4mm silk ribbon
Chenille #22 needle

E1

Ruched rose (page 78)
4mm silk ribbon
Chenille #22 needle

H3

Simple beaded button (page 91)
Nymo thread
Milliners #10 needle

E2

Stab/straight stitch (page 73)
1 strand DMC thread
Milliners #7 needle

G1

Beaded sequin (page 83)
Nymo thread
Milliners #10 needle

E3

Ribbon stitch (page 77)
4mm silk ribbon
Chenille #22 needle

G2

Stab/straight stitch (page 73)
1 strand rayon thread
Milliners #7 needle

H4

Lazy daisy/detached chain
stitch (page 72)
Perle cotton #8 thread
Milliners #4 needle

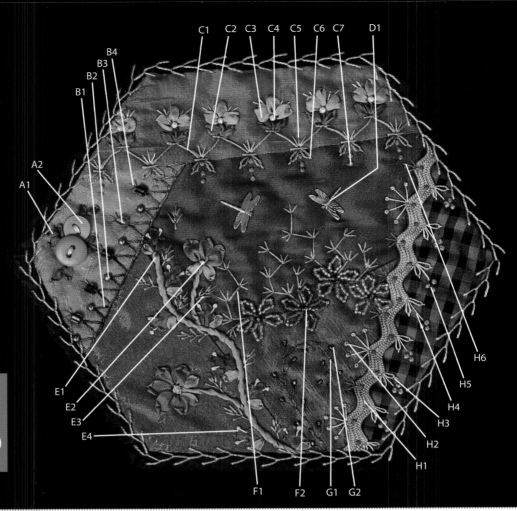

B1
B2
B3
B4

C1 C2 C3 C4 C5 C6 C7 D1

A2
A1

E1
E2
E3
E4

F1 F2 G1 G2

H1
H2
H3
H4
H5
H6

Hexagon 24

(Pattern 8, page 109)

A1

Ribbon stitch (page 77)
4mm silk ribbon
Chenille #22 needle

A2

Button (page 90)
Perle cotton #8 thread
Milliners #4 needle

B1

Closed buttonhole/blanket
stitch (page 71)
Twisted silk thread
Chenille #22 needle

B2

Single-bead stitch (page 85)
Nymo thread
Milliners #10 needle

B3

Single-bead stitch (page 85)
Nymo thread
Milliners #10 needle

B4

Stab/straight stitch (page 73)
1 strand DMC thread
Milliners #7 needle

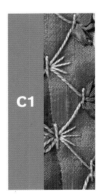

C1

Chevron stitch (page 71)
Perle cotton #8 thread
Milliners #4 needle

C2

Lazy daisy/detached chain
stitch—silk ribbon (page 76)
4mm silk ribbon
Chenille #22 needle

C3

Padded stab stitch (page 77)

7mm silk ribbon and perle cotton #8 thread

Chenille #22 and milliners #4 needles

E2

Ribbon stitch flower (page 77)

4mm silk ribbon

Chenille #22 needle

H1

Couched rickrack (page 90) with colonial knots (page 71)

Perle cotton #12 thread

Milliners #7 needle

C4

Single-bead stitch (page 85)

Nymo thread

Milliners #10 needle

E3

Fly stitch (page 72)

1 strand rayon thread

Milliners #7 needle

H2

Pistil stitch (page 73)

Perle cotton #12 thread

Milliners #7 needle

C5

Stab/straight stitch (page 73)

Perle cotton #12 thread

Milliners #7 needle

E4

Pistil stitch (page 73)

Perle cotton #12 thread

Milliners #7 needle

H3

Lazy daisy/detached chain stitch (page 72)

Perle cotton #12 thread

Milliners #7 needle

C6

Lazy daisy/detached chain stitch (page 72)

Perle cotton #8 thread

Milliners #4 needle

F1

Stab/straight stitch (page 73)

1 strand rayon thread

Milliners #7 needle

H4

Stab/straight stitch (page 73)

Perle cotton #12 thread

Milliners #7 needle

C7

Colonial knot (page 71)

Perle cotton #8 thread

Milliners #4 needle

F2

Beaded rounded petal (page 83)

Nymo thread

Beading needle

H5

Colonial knot (page 71)

Perle cotton #8 thread

Milliners #4 needle

D1

Charm (page 90)

Nymo thread

Milliners #10 needle

G1

Feather stitch (page 72)

1 strand rayon thread

Milliners #7 needle

H6

Stab/straight stitch (page 73)

Perle cotton #12 thread

Milliners #7 needle

E1

Whipped chain stitch (page 79)

4mm silk ribbon and perle cotton #12 thread

Chenille #22 and milliners #7 needles

G2

Single-bead stitch (page 85)

Nymo thread

Milliners #10 needle

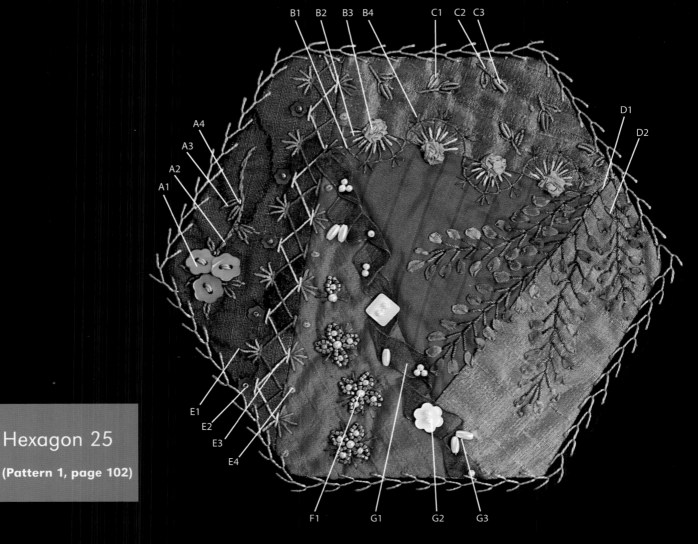

Hexagon 25

(Pattern 1, page 102)

A1

Button cluster (page 90)
Perle cotton #8 thread
Milliners #4 needle

A2

Stem stitch (page 73)
Perle cotton #8 thread
Milliners #4 needle

A3

Lazy daisy / detached chain
stitch (page 72)
Perle cotton #8 thread
Milliners #4 needle

A4

Single-bead stitch (page 85)
Nymo thread
Milliners #10 needle

B1

Buttonhole/blanket stitch fan (page 70)
Perle cotton #12 thread
Milliners #7 needle

B2

Stab/straight stitch (page 73)
Perle cotton #12 thread
Milliners #7 needle

B3

Ruched rose (page 78)
7mm silk ribbon
Chenille #22 needle

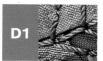

D1

Fly stitch (page 72)
Twisted silk thread
Chenille #22 needle

E4

Colonial knot (page 71)
Perle cotton #8 thread
Milliners #4 needle

B4

Stab/straight stitch (page 73)
1 strand rayon thread
Milliners #7 needle

D2

Ribbon stitch (page 77)
4mm silk ribbon
Chenille #22 needle

F1

Beaded daisy (page 81)
Nymo thread and 1 strand rayon thread
Beading needle and milliners #7 needle

C1

Lazy daisy/detached chain
stitch (page 72)
Twisted silk thread
Chenille #22 needle

E1

Stab/straight stitch (page 73)
Twisted rayon thread
Chenille #22 needle

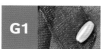

G1

Couched ribbon garland (page 90)
11mm organza ribbon and Nymo thread
Chenille #22 and milliners #10 needles

C2

Fly stitch (page 72)
Twisted silk thread
Chenille #22 needle

E2

Beaded sequin (page 83)
Nymo thread
Milliners #10 needle

G2

Simple beaded button (page 91)
Nymo thread
Milliners #10 needle

C3

Bullion knot (page 70)
Twisted silk thread
Milliners #4 needle

E3

Chevron stitch (page 71)
Perle cotton #8 thread
Milliners #4 needle

G3

Single-bead stitch (page 85)
Nymo thread
Milliners #10 needle

Relax—don't make the stitches too tight or the detail will disappear, but do try to make them even! Crazy quilting is worked on a foundation fabric, so a small knot to begin and end the stitches is perfectly acceptable.

Alternating Chain Stitch

1. Thread a chenille #22 needle with 2 contrasting threads.

2. Bring the needle to the surface of the work at A.

3. Insert the needle from B to C. Keep a thread under the needle and the other thread above.

4. Pull the needle and both threads through.

5. Form another chain stitch but swap the thread that remains under the needle.

6. Pull both threads through.

7. Continue as desired.

Bullion Knot Flower

1. Begin by marking a small circle with an erasable pencil where the flower center will be.

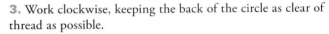

2. Make a series of bullion knot petals around the outside of the marked circle.

3. Work clockwise, keeping the back of the circle as clear of thread as possible.

4. Add colonial knots (page 71) or beads to the center of the flower.

Bullion Knot

1. Bring the needle to the surface of the work at A.

2. Reinsert at B (the distance between A and B will be the length of the bullion knot).

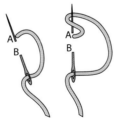

3. Emerge at A but do not pull the needle all the way through the fabric.

4. Wrap the working thread around the needle as many times as required to equal the size of the backstitch.

5. Support the wraps on the needle with your thumb and index finger, and pull the needle through. Pull the thread away from and then toward you.

6. With the wraps evenly packed on the thread, reinsert the needle at B to end the bullion knot.

Buttonhole/Blanket Stitch Fan or Pinwheel Stitch

1. With an erasable pencil, mark the desired shape onto the work.

2. Bring the needle to the surface of the work at A.

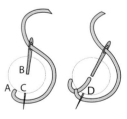

3. Reinsert at B.

4. With the thread under the needle, emerge at C.

5. Reinsert the needle at B and emerge at D with the thread under the needle.

6. Continue until fan or pinwheel is complete.

7. Finish with a small anchoring stitch.

Chain Feather Stitch

1. Work a single chain as described in chain stitch (below).

2. Reinsert the needle at D so that A-C-D forms a straight line.

3. Emerge at E, which is at an angle to the previous line.

4. Work a single chain from E to D.

5. Reinsert at F so that E-D-F forms a straight line.

6. Emerge at G, which is at an angle to the previous line.

7. Continue as required. End with a small anchoring stitch.

Chain Stitch

1. Bring the needle to the surface of the work at A.

2. Loop the thread to the right and reinsert at B.

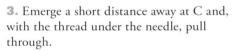

3. Emerge a short distance away at C and, with the thread under the needle, pull through.

4. Loop the thread to the right and insert the needle exactly where the thread emerged in the previous loop.

5. Continue as desired, finishing with a small anchoring stitch over the last loop.

Chevron Stitch

1. Bring the needle to the surface of the work at A and insert to the right at B; exit half a stitch length to the left, at C.

2. Insert the needle at D and exit half a stitch length to the left, at E.

3. Insert the needle a stitch length to the right at F, and exit a half stitch to the left at G.

4. Continue as desired.

Closed Buttonhole/Blanket Stitch

1. Work from left to right.

2. Keep each sloping stitch the same slope and length.

3. Bring the needle to the surface of the work at A.

4. Sloping to the right, reinsert at B.

5. With the thread under the needle, emerge at C.

6. With the thread under the needle and sloping to the right, reinsert at B and emerge at D.

7. Continue as desired, finishing with a small anchoring stitch.

Colonial Knot

1. Bring the thread to the surface of the work at A.

2. Cross the thread over the needle from left to right. Wrap the thread under the needle and then around the needle from right to left (creating a figure 8 on the needle).

3. Reinsert the needle close to where it originally emerged.

4. Hold the needle in place and gently pull the working thread taut toward the surface of the work.

5. A firm knot will form. Pull the needle through to the back of the work.

Cretan and Herringbone Stitch Combination

1. Bring the needle to the surface of the work at A.

2. With the thread under the needle, insert at B and emerge at C.

3. Insert the needle at D and emerge at E.

4. Repeat to the desired length.

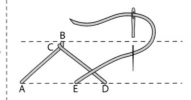

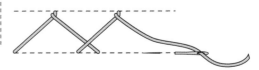

Cretan Stitch

1. Bring the needle to the surface of the work at A.

2. Loop the working thread to the right and reinsert at B.

3. With the thread under the needle, emerge at C.

4. Loop the thread to the right and reinsert at D.

5. With the thread under the needle, emerge at E.

6. Continue as required.

Feather Stitch

1. Bring the needle to the surface of the work at A.

2. Loop the thread to the left and insert at B (in line with A).

3. With the thread under the needle, emerge at C (between A and B, forming a V shape).

4. Insert at D. Loop the thread to the right and emerge at E.

5. Alternate the stitches from left to right. Continue as desired, finishing with a small stitch over the last loop.

Fern Stitch

1. Bring the needle to the surface of the work at A.

2. Reinsert at B and reemerge at A.

3. Insert at C and reemerge at A to complete the left-hand stitch.

4. Then insert the needle at D and emerge at E to complete the right-hand stitch and set up for the next group.

5. The 3 stitches that make up a fern stitch are usually the same length.

Fly Stitch

1. Bring the needle to the surface of the work at A.

2. Insert at B and, with the thread under the needle, emerge at C.

3. Reinsert at D to form the anchor stitch.

4. Extended fly stitch has a longer anchoring stitch.

Fly Stitch Leaf

1. Begin by drawing a small leaf shape onto the fabric.

2. The leaf is made up of a series of fly stitches that progressively get larger to suit the shape of the leaf.

3. The first fly stitch is made at the tip of the leaf shape.

4. To complete the leaf, make a small stab/straight stitch (page 73) in the middle of the first fly stitch.

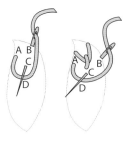

Herringbone Stitch

1. Bring the needle to the surface of the work at A.

2. Insert at B.

3. Emerge at C (to the left of B).

4. Reinsert at D (to the right of B).

5. Emerge at E (to the left of D).

6. Continue as desired.

I like to make a small horizontal couching stitch where the 2 threads cross.

Lazy Daisy / Detached Chain Stitch

1. Bring the needle to the surface of the work at A.

2. Make a loop with the thread.

3. Hold the loop down with your non-working hand, reinsert the needle where it first emerged at B, and emerge a short distance away, at C.

4. With the thread under the needle, make a small stitch from C to D to anchor the loop.

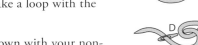
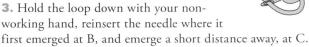

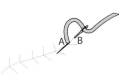

Pistil Stitch

1. A pistil stitch is a stab/straight stitch (below) with an attached French knot.

2. Bring the needle to the surface of the work at A and wrap the thread around the needle 2 or 3 times. Hold the thread taut and reinsert at B. Pull the needle though.

Stab/Straight Stitch

1. Bring the needle to the surface of the work at A, and work a stitch to B in the required length and direction.

2. Do not make stab/straight stitches too long because they tend to catch.

3. A twisted thread is best for this stitch.

Stem Stitch

1. Work from right to left and keep the thread below the needle.

2. Bring the needle to the surface of the work at A. Reinsert at B.

3. Emerge at C (halfway between A and B).

4. Reinsert at D and emerge at E, beside B above the line of stitching.

5. Continue as desired.

Straight Feather Stitch

1. This stitch is worked in the same manner as the feather stitch (page 72), except that the "spine" of the feather stays relatively straight.

2. Bring the needle to the surface of the work at A.

3. Loop the thread to the left and reinsert at B.

4. With the thread under the needle, emerge at C (under A).

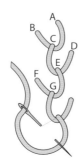

Wheatear Stitch

1. Work 2 stab/straight stitches (at left) at A and B, and then at C and D.

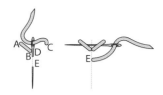

2. Bring the thread through below these stitches at E.

3. Pass the needle under the 2 stab/straight stitches without entering the fabric.

4. Reinsert at F.

5. Emerge at G to begin the next series of stitches.

Whipped Herringbone Stitch

1. Complete a length of herringbone stitches (page 72).

2. Bring the needle to the surface of the work at A.

3. Staying on the surface, pass the blunt end of the needle under the right-hand side of the first stitch. Pull the thread through and pass the needle under the left side of the second stitch. Continue the length of the herringbone stitches, making sure to keep the tension of the whipping stitch relaxed.

4. Insert the needle to the back of the work and fasten off.

5. Loop the thread to the right and reinsert at D.

6. With the thread under the needle, emerge at E.

7. Loop the thread to the left and reinsert at F.

8. With the thread under the needle, emerge at G.

9. Repeat to the right.

10. Finish with a small stitch over the last loop.

Woven Spider Web

1. Make 8 evenly spaced spokes: With an erasable pencil, draw a circle the size you want the finished web. With stab stitches, create spokes by stitching from A to B, C to D, E to F, and G to H.

2. Bring the needle to the surface of the work in the center of the spokes.

3. With the blunt end of the needle, go over the spoke to the right and then under it, and under the next spoke to the left.

4. Pull the thread toward the center.

5. Go back over the spoke you just went under, and then under it and under the next spoke to the left.

6. Continue working counterclockwise until the desired fullness has been reached. You are wrapping the thread around each spoke as you go.

7. Finish on the wrong side of the work with a small anchoring stitch.

Zigzag Chain Stitch

1. This stitch is worked in the same way as a chain stitch (page 71), except that you are splitting the thread of the first chain link when you start the second link.

2. Angle the first link to the left and the second to the right.

3. Continue as desired.

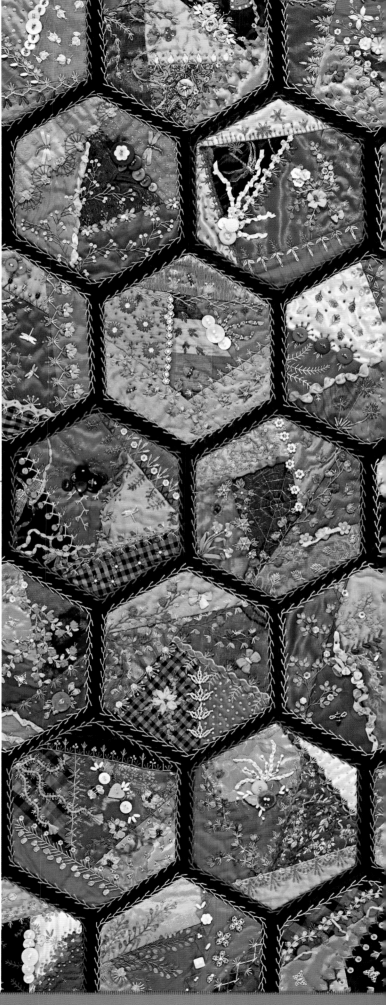

7 *Silk Ribbon Stitches*

Threading and Knotting

A chenille needle is used in all silk ribbon embroidery.

Threading the Needle

1. Cut a 10″–12″ length of ribbon.

2. Thread an end of the ribbon through the eye of the needle.

3. Turn the point of the needle and pierce the threaded end of ribbon.

4. Hold the point of the needle and pull the long end of the ribbon down, allowing the ribbon to "lock" over the eye.

Knotting the Ribbon

1. Make a ¼″ fold at the end of the ribbon.

2. Pierce the fold with the point of the needle.

3. Pull it down over the needle to form a soft knot at the end.

Fastening Off

1. Using the blunt end of the needle, pass the ribbon under the back of a previously worked stitch.

2. Form a loop with the ribbon and pass the needle through the loop.

3. Gently pull the ribbon until the knot is tight.

tip

It is very important to keep the ribbon on the back of the work untwisted. This will allow it to fan out on the surface of the work.

Bent Stab Stitch

1. This stitch is perfect for a leaf.

2. Bring the ribbon to the surface of the work at A.

3. With a single strand of matching floss, tack the ribbon to the work at the desired distance from A, at B.

4. Fold the ribbon forward and reinsert at the desired location, C.

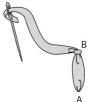

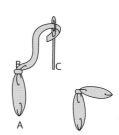

Coral Stitch

1. Work from right to left. Bring the ribbon to the surface of the work at A.

2. Lay the ribbon along the design line.

3. Secure the ribbon with the thumb of your nonworking hand.

4. Loop the ribbon to the right and take a small stitch under the ribbon from B to C.

5. With the ribbon under the needle, pull through.

6. Continue as desired. Stitch the ribbon down on the wrong side of the work to end.

7. The segments of ribbon between the knots may be smooth or raised.

8. Keep the tension loose.

Fishbone Stitch

1. Using an erasable pencil, draw a small leaf shape with a line down the center.

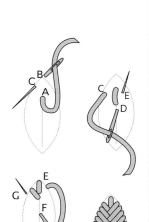

2. Begin below the tip of the leaf and make a small stab stitch (page 79) from A to B, ensuring that the ribbon is not twisted.

3. Emerge at C, reinsert at D, and then emerge at E. Insert again at F and emerge at G.

4. Continue until the leaf shape is filled.

Lazy Daisy / Detached Chain Stitch—Silk Ribbon

1. Bring the ribbon to the surface of the work.

2. Make a loop with the ribbon. Hold the loop down on the surface of the work with your nonworking hand and reinsert at the point where the needle originally emerged.

3. Emerge a short distance away and secure the top of the loop by making a stab stitch (page 79). Keep the tension of the ribbon relaxed.

4. Refer to the illustrations for lazy daisy / detached chain stitch in the embroidery stitch section (page 72); this stitch is made the same way.

Lazy Daisy / Detached Chain Stitch Flower

1. Begin by marking a small circle with an erasable pencil where the flower center will be.

Flower

2. Make a series of lazy daisy / detached chain stitch (above) petals around the outside of the marked circle.

3. Work clockwise, keeping the back of the circle clear of any silk ribbon.

4. Keep the tension of the lazy daisies / detached chains relaxed.

5. Add colonial knots (page 71) or beads to the center.

Loop Stitch with Colonial Knot or Bead

1. This stitch is a loop stitch anchored in the middle with a colonial knot or a bead.

2. Form a single loop stitch (page 77).

3. Emerge through the base of the loop.

4. Form a colonial knot (page 71) or attach a bead. Secure the ribbon on the wrong side of the work to end.

Loop Stitch and Flower

1. Bring the ribbon to the surface of the work at A.

2. Make a tiny back-stitch and reinsert at B.

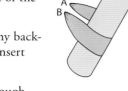

3. Place a pencil or straw through the ribbon loop and, keeping the ribbon untwisted, gently pull the ribbon through the loop, over the pencil. Remove the pencil once the ribbon is taut.

4. Repeat for the next loop stitch. Secure the ribbon on the wrong side of the work to end.

5. To make a loop stitch flower, mark a small circle with an erasable pencil where the flower center will be.

6. Make a series of loop stitch petals around the outside of the marked circle.

7. Work clockwise, keeping the back of the marked circle clear of any silk ribbon.

8. Add colonial knots (page 71) or beads to the center of the flower.

Padded Stab Stitch

1. Bring the ribbon to the surface of the work and make a colonial knot (page 71).

2. Form a stab stitch (page 79) over the colonial knot.

3. Keep the tension of the stab stitch relaxed.

4. Secure the ribbon on the wrong side of the work to end.

Plume Stitch

1. Work this stitch toward you; begin where you would like the plume stitch to end.

2. Mark the fabric with a temporary guideline.

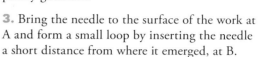

3. Bring the needle to the surface of the work at A and form a small loop by inserting the needle a short distance from where it emerged, at B.

4. Emerge through the base of the previous loop, at C.

5. Keep the ribbon untwisted as you work the series of loops.

6. Stitch the ribbon down on the wrong side of the work to end.

Ribbon Stitch

1. Bring the ribbon to the surface of the work at A.

2. Lay the ribbon flat and insert the needle through the ribbon where you want the tip of the stitch to be.

3. Pull the ribbon gently through the work.

4. The ribbon will curl inward to form a point (be careful not to pull too tightly).

5. Secure the ribbon on the wrong side of the work to end.

Ribbon Stitch Flower

1. Begin by marking a small circle with an erasable pencil where the flower center will be.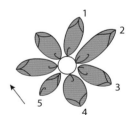

2. Make a series of ribbon stitch (above) petals around the outside of the marked circle.

3. Work clockwise, keeping the back of the marked circle clear of any silk ribbon.

4. Add colonial knots (page 71) or seed beads for the center of the flower.

5. Keep the tension relaxed and the ribbon untwisted.

Ruched Rose

1. Bring the ribbon to the surface of the work at A.

2. Hold the ribbon in your nonworking hand approximately 3″ away from the surface. Form a colonial knot (page 71).

3. Keeping the knot on the needle, form small gathering stitches along the length of the ribbon.

4. Once you reach the end of the ribbon, reinsert the needle into the work at B. Gently pull the ribbon through.

5. A small rose will form.

6. Secure the ribbon on the wrong side of the work to end.

tip

A variegated silk ribbon will give the rose shading without your having to change the ribbon during the stitching.

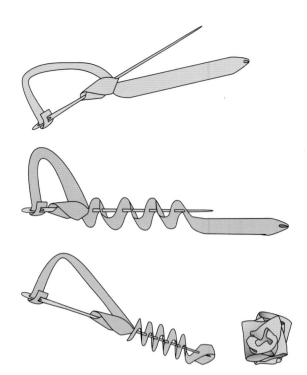

Ruched Silk Ribbon Garland

1. Thread a milliner's needle with a single strand of embroidery thread to match the silk ribbon.

2. Bring the ribbon to the surface of the work.

3. Bring the embroidery thread to the surface of the work a short distance from where the ribbon first emerged.

4. Form a number of small gathering stitches along the middle of the ribbon with the embroidery thread.

5. The last gathering stitch should end with the thread on the underside of the ribbon.

6. Reinsert the embroidery thread into the work alongside where it emerged.

7. Gently pull the thread through the work; a small rose will form on the surface of the work.

8. Form an anchoring knot on the wrong side of the work.

9. Continue as desired; don't bring the ribbon to the back between roses. Reinsert the ribbon and secure on the wrong side of the work to end.

10. These garlands may be formed into geometric shapes, zigzags, or gentle folds.

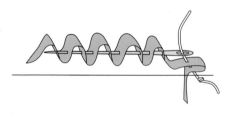

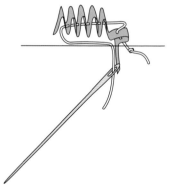

Spider Web Rose

1. With an erasable pencil, mark a temporary circle with 5 evenly spaced spokes.

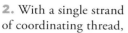

2. With a single strand of coordinating thread, make a fly stitch (page 72) to create the first 3 spokes and then stab/straight stitches (page 73) for the other 2 spokes.

3. Bring the ribbon to the surface of the work at the center of the spokes.

4. With the blunt end of the needle, weave the ribbon over and under the spokes, allowing the ribbon to twist.

5. Continue until the rose is full. Reinsert the needle to make the final petal.

6. Secure the ribbon on the back of the work to end.

7. Keep the weaving soft and loose.

8. Add seed beads or colonial knots (page 71) for the center of the rose.

Split Stitch

1. Bring the needle to the surface of the work at A.

2. Loosely lay the ribbon flat on the surface of the work. Reinsert the needle at B (about ⅜" from A).

3. Emerge at C, splitting the ribbon, and gently pull through.

4. Repeat for desired length.

Stab Stitch—Silk Ribbon

1. Bring the ribbon to the surface of the work at A.

2. Use the nose of small scissors to keep the ribbon from twisting, and reinsert at B.

3. Gently pull the ribbon through the fabric.

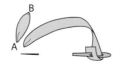

Twisted Stab Stitch

1. Bring the needle to the surface of the work at A.

2. Twist the ribbon as many times as desired.

3. Reinsert at B.

4. Keep the tension of the ribbon relaxed.

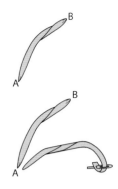

Whipped Chain Stitch

1. Work a foundation row of chain stitches (page 71).

2. Bring the ribbon to the surface at the start of the foundation chain.

3. With the blunt end of the needle and staying on the surface of the work, pass the ribbon over and under each link of the chain.

4. Reinsert at the end of the last chain stitch and secure to end.

5. Keep the tension of the whipstitch relaxed and the ribbon untwisted.

Whipped Stab Stitch

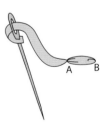

1. This stitch combination is perfect for the bodies of butterflies.

2. Make a single stab stitch (at left) from A to B. Bring the needle to the surface of the work at A.

3. With the blunt end of the needle, wrap the stab stitch until completely full. Reinsert at B. Stitch down on the wrong side of the work to end.

4. Keep the ribbon untwisted during the wrapping of the stab stitch.

A Few Points to Keep in Mind

- It is advisable to use a hoop while beading.

- Begin and end beading securely with anchoring knots.

- The beading thread should match the bead, not the fabric.

- Unless otherwise instructed, always insert the needle into the fabric at 90°, not at an angle.

- Knot before and after every bead or sequin.

- Make sure the beads are firm on the work—there is nothing worse than a wobbly bead!

- Try to buy good-quality beads—some beads are not durable and in time will lose their color.

- Beads need to be of a bolder color than you might think. Because they are tiny, they need to contrast strongly against the fabrics in order to show up on the work.

- Anything with a hole in it is a bead!

- Beads catch the light and add a lovely sense of movement to crazy quilts.

- Any time you think of adding a bullion stitch or colonial knot, try adding a bugle or seed bead instead.

- To prevent fabric from puckering under the beads, do not have the traveling thread longer than 1″.

tip

Do not bead within ½″ of the perimeter of a hexagon. Tack the beads that you will need to complete the seam treatments onto the muslin for safekeeping.

Beaded Backstitch

1. When securing a continuous line of beads, it is very important to follow this procedure.

- Beads
- Nymo thread
- Beading needle

2. Bring the needle to the surface of the work and pick up 3 beads.

3. Snug the beads up against each other and insert the needle into the fabric at the end of the third bead. Emerge between the first and second beads.

4. Travel through beads 2 and 3, and then pick up 3 more beads.

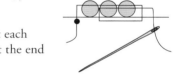

5. Snug the beads up against each other and insert the needle at the end of the last bead.

6. Continue until desired length is reached. Finish with an anchoring knot.

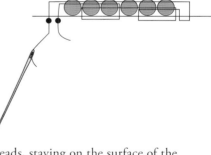

7. To straighten and smooth the line of beads, pass the needle and thread through the entire length of beads, staying on the surface of the fabric. Once the end of the beading has been reached, reinsert the needle to the wrong side of the fabric and finish off.

Beaded Bee

1. Follow the diagram for the bee body, and use the beaded backstitch (page 80) method to secure the body beads.

- Beads
- Nymo thread
- Beading needle

2. For the wings, bring the needle to the surface of the work next to the first black beaded stripe of the body.

3. Pick up 11 beads and reinsert through the first picked-up bead, so that the wings are attached to the fabric only at their bases.

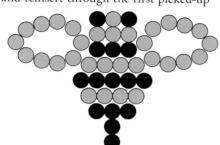

4. Finish with an anchoring knot.

5. Repeat for the other side.

Beaded Chain

1. Bring the needle to the surface of the work and pick up enough beads to cover the desired size of the loop, but make sure it is an odd number of beads.

- Beads
- Nymo thread
- Milliners #10 needle

2. Come back through bead 1 and reinsert at the starting point.

3. Emerge in the center of the previously made loop and pick up the same number of beads as in the first loop.

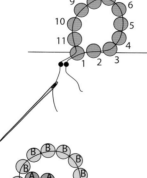

4. Continue for the desired length of the chain.

5. Finish with an anchoring stitch.

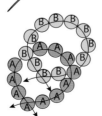

Beaded Daisy

1. Attach a round pearl bead to the fabric; this will form the center of the daisy.

- Beads
- Nymo thread and 1 strand of rayon thread
- Beading needle and milliners #7 needle

2. Bring the needle to the surface of the work alongside the pearl bead.

3. Pick up 5 beads.

4. Reinsert the needle into the fabric and form an anchoring knot.

5. Repeat with another row of beads parallel to the first.

6. Emerge in the center of the parallel row of beads.

7. Pick up a round pearl bead and insert within the parallel lines.

8. This forms a petal of the daisy.

9. Continue with the desired number of petals.

10. Add stab/straight stitches (page 73) for added detail.

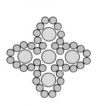

Beaded Feather Stitch

1. Bring the needle to the surface of the work at A and pick up an even number of beads.

- Beads
- Nymo thread
- Beading needle

2. Allow the beads on the thread to form a V shape.

3. Reinsert to the right of the starting point at B.

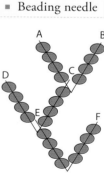

4. With the needle over the thread, emerge at the bottom of the V (make sure that each side of the V has an equal number of beads) at C.

5. Repeat to the left.

6. Continue alternating from left to right for the desired length of the feather stitching.

7. Finish with an anchoring knot.

Beaded Forget-Me-Not

1. The forget-me-not flower is made and then couched onto the surface of the work.

- Beads
- Nymo thread
- Milliners #10 needle

2. Thread a beading needle with approximately 12″ of Nymo thread. Pick up 6 pearl or round beads.

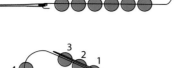

3. Pass the needle through the first 3 beads to form a circle with the thread.

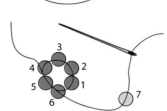

4. Pick up a bead of a different color.

5. Pass the needle though the sixth pearl bead.

6. Pull both threads firmly so the center bead sits in the middle of the pearl beads.

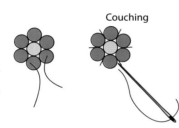

Couching

7. Knot the threads tightly.

8. Using a thread from the knot, couch the flower to the surface of the work.

9. Pass the remaining thread to the back of the work and form an anchoring knot.

Beaded Grapes

1. Bring the needle to the surface of the work at A (this will be the top of the bunch of grapes).

- Beads
- Nymo thread
- Milliners #10 needle

2. Follow the diagram for placement of beads.

3. Use the beaded backstitch (page 80) method to form the tiers of grapes.

4. Finish with an anchoring stitch.

Beaded Pointed Petal/Leaf

1. Bring the needle to the surface of the work and pick up 9 seed beads.

- Beads
- Nymo thread
- Beading needle

2. Hold the last picked-up bead (#9) between thumb and index finger.

3. Pass the needle through the next 2 beads (#8 and #7) on the thread.

4. Pick up 5 more beads and insert the needle through the last bead (#1) and into the fabric.

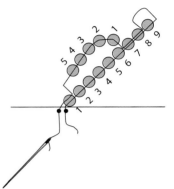

5. Finish with an anchoring knot on the wrong side of the fabric.

6. To anchor the petal, lay it flat on the surface of the work.

7. Bring the needle to the surface in line with the last bead (#9) of the petal.

Couching

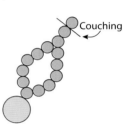

8. Couch down by stitching over the beading thread of the petal.

9. Finish with an anchoring stitch.

Beaded Rounded Petal

1. Bring the needle to the surface of the work and pick up

- Beads
- Nymo thread
- Beading needle

10 seed beads (increase the number of beads if a larger petal is desired, but always use an even number).

2. Insert the needle through the first picked-up bead and then into the fabric.

3. Form an anchoring knot on the wrong side of the fabric.

4. Lay the petal flat and bring the thread up below the middle bead of the rounded petal.

5. Pass the needle through the middle bead and back down to the wrong side of the fabric. Finish with an anchoring stitch.

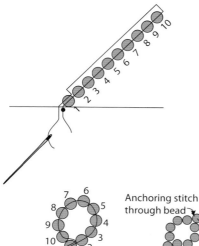

Anchoring stitch through bead

Beaded Sequin

1. Bring the needle to the surface of the work and pick up a sequin and a seed bead.

- Sequin
- Bead
- Nymo thread
- Milliners #10 needle

2. Hold the seed bead between the thumb and index finger, and reinsert the needle through the sequin.

3. The seed bead will now hold the sequin in place.

4. Finish with an anchoring knot on the wrong side of the fabric under the sequin before traveling along to the next sequin.

5. Alternatively, a sequin *without a bead* can be simply couched down with matching Nymo thread.

Beaded Tassel

1. Bring the needle to the surface of the work.

- Beads
- Nymo thread
- Milliners #10 needle

2. Pick up a combination of beads for desired length of tassel.

3. Hold the last bead between thumb and index finger, and reinsert the needle through all the other beads on the thread.

4. Finish with an anchoring knot. Add more tassels as desired.

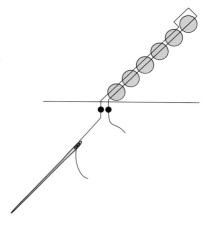

Bugle Bead Leaf

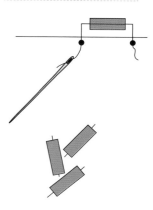

1. Bring the needle to the surface of the work and pick up a bugle bead.

- Bugle beads
- Nymo thread
- Milliners #10 needle

2. Reinsert at a slight angle. Form an anchoring knot.

3. Emerge midway and to the side of the first bugle.

4. Reinsert at a slight angle.

5. Form an anchoring knot.

6. Continue for desired length.

7. Finish with an anchoring knot.

Bugle Fan

- Round bead or 4mm silk ribbon
- Bugle beads
- Nymo thread
- Milliners #10 needle

1. Bring the needle to the surface of the work, and pick up and secure a round bead.

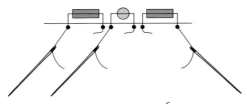

2. Emerge on the right-hand side of the bead and pick up a bugle bead.

3. Reinsert into the work and form an anchoring knot.

4. Continue with the desired number of bugle beads to form a fan shape.

5. The center bead may be replaced with a colonial knot (page 71) in 4mm silk ribbon.

Bugle and Seed Bead Chain

1. Bring the needle to the surface of the work.

- Bugle and round or seed beads
- Nymo thread
- Beading needle

2. Pick up a bugle bead and then 11 round beads.

3. Pass the needle back through the bugle bead to the wrong side of the fabric.

4. Form an anchoring stitch.

5. Lay the bugle link flat and bring the thread up in the center of the beaded loop to continue with the next loop of the chain.

6. Finish the last loop of the chain with an anchoring stitch.

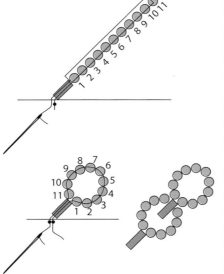

Daisy Chain

1. Bring the needle to the surface and pick up the desired number of beads.

- Beads
- Nymo thread
- Beading needle

2. Return the needle to the fabric at the starting point, forming a loop with the beads.

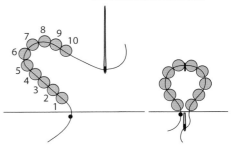

3. Emerge inside the loop near the top. Pick up the same number of beads to form the next loop in the chain.

4. Continue as desired, ending with an anchoring stitch over the last chain.

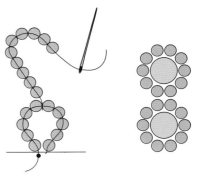

5. Bring the needle to the surface of the work in the middle of the first link.

6. Pick up a pearl bead and reinsert the needle within the loop.

7. Form an anchoring stitch on the wrong side of the pearl bead. Continue for each link in the chain.

Sequin Fun

- Sequin
- 1 strand rayon thread
- Milliners #7 needle

- Sequin
- Perle cotton #12 thread
- Milliners #7 needle

1. Bring the needle to the surface of the work through a sequin.

2. Form a series of evenly spaced stab/straight stitches (page 73) radiating from the center of the sequin.

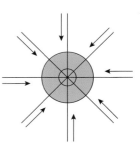

3. Form a colonial knot (page 71) between the spokes, if desired.

4. Finish with an anchoring knot.

Single-Bead Stitch

1. When attaching a single bead of any size, bring the thread from the back to the front.

2. Put the bead on the needle and reinsert the needle into the fabric to the back of the work. Form an anchoring knot to end.

- Seed bead
- Nymo thread
- Milliners #10 needle

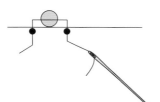

Upright Bugle Beads

1. Bring the needle to the surface of the work, and pick up a bugle bead and a seed bead.

2. Hold the seed bead between your thumb and forefinger, and reinsert the needle through the bugle bead.

3. Pull the thread taut.

4. Finish with an anchoring stitch.

- Bugle beads
- Seed beads
- Nymo thread
- Milliners #10 needle

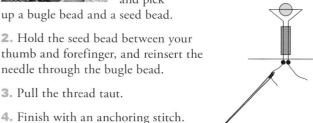

String of Beads

1. Thread the desired number of beads onto a length of Nymo thread.

- Beads
- Nymo thread
- Beading needle

2. Weave the strand of beads over and under a length of ruched silk ribbon garland (page 78).

Upright Bugle Beads and Beaded Tassel

Follow the instructions for upright bugle beads (above) and beaded tassel (page 83).

- Bugle beads
- Round or seed beads
- Nymo thread
- Beading needle

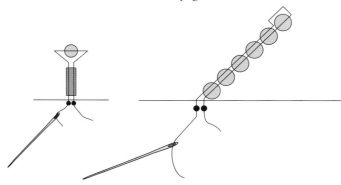

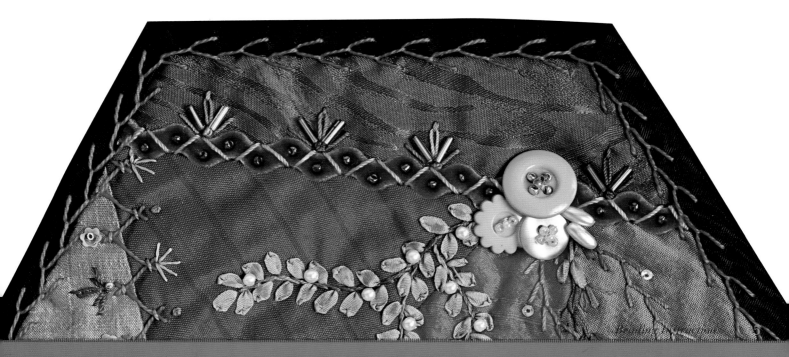

9 Insects, Webs, and Miscellaneous Embroidery

Agapanthus

Stem:
- Stem stitch (page 73)
- 1 strand rayon thread
- Milliners #7 needle

Flower:
- Fly stitch (page 72) and stab/straight stitch (page 73)
- 1 strand rayon thread
- Milliners #7 needle

Leaves:
- Bugle beads
- Nymo thread
- Milliners #10 needle

Dragonfly

Body and head:
- Beaded backstitch (page 80)
- Nymo thread
- Beading needle

Wings:
- Ribbon stitch (page 77)
- 4mm or 7mm silk ribbon
- Chenille #22 needle

The body of the dragonfly may be made of round or bugle beads. A larger round bead is used for the head.

Delphinium

Stem:
- Stem stitch (page 73)
- Perle cotton #12 thread
- Milliners #7 needle

Leaves:
- Ribbon stitch (page 77)
- 7mm silk ribbon
- Milliners #22 needle

Petals:
- Ribbon stitch (page 77)
- 4mm silk ribbon
- Chenille #22 needle

Buds:
- Colonial knot (page 71)
- 4mm silk ribbon
- Chenille #22 needle

Petals | Buds
Leaves
Leaves

Fuchsia

1. Stitch the fuchsia petals in numerical order as noted on the illustration.

2. Add stem, buds, and leaves as desired.

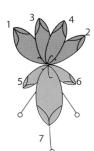

Stem:
- Whipped chain stitch (page 79)
- Perle cotton #12 thread and 4mm silk ribbon
- Milliners #7 and chenille #22 needles

Petals:
- Ribbon stitch (page 77)
- 4mm silk ribbon
- Chenille #22 needle

Pistils:
- Pistil stitch (page 73)
- Perle cotton #12 thread
- Milliners #7 needle

Leaves:
- Ribbon stitch (page 77)
- 4mm silk ribbon
- Chenille #22 needle

Buds:
- Stab stitch (page 79)
- 4mm silk ribbon
- Chenille #22 needle

Lazy Daisy / Detached Chain Bud

Bud:
- Lazy daisy / detached chain stitch— silk ribbon (page 76)
- 4mm silk ribbon or 4mm organza ribbon
- Chenille #22 needle

Leaves:
- Stab/straight stitch (page 73)
- Perle cotton #12 thread
- Milliners #7 needle

Lazy Daisy / Detached Chain Butterfly

Body:
- Bullion knot (page 70)
- Twisted silk thread
- Milliners #4 needle

Wings:
- Lazy daisy / detached chain stitch (page 72) with optional stab/ straight stitches (page 73)
- Twisted silk thread
- Chenille #22 needle

Antennae:
- Pistil stitch (page 73)
- Twisted silk thread
- Chenille #22 needle

tip

A variegated thread will add color to the butterfly without your having to change threads.

Lazy Daisy / Detached Chain Ribbon Butterfly

Body:
- Padded stab stitch (page 77)
- 4mm silk ribbon
- Chenille #22 needle

Head:
- Colonial knot (page 71)
- 4mm silk ribbon
- Chenille #22 needle

Wings:
- Lazy daisy / detached chain stitch— silk ribbon (page 76)
- 4mm silk ribbon
- Chenille #22 needle

Antennae:
- Pistil stitch (page 73)
- 1 strand DMC thread
- Milliners #7 needle

Loop Stitch Butterfly

Body:
- Whipped stab stitch (page 79)
- 4mm silk ribbon
- Chenille #22 needle

Wings:
- Loop stitch (page 77, Steps 1–4)
- 7mm silk ribbon
- Chenille #22 needle

Antennae:
- Stab/straight stitch (page 73)
- Twisted silk thread
- Chenille #22 needle

Rosebud

There are many variations of the rosebud; try to mix and match the stitches to get a variety.

Bud:
- Lazy daisy / detached chain stitch—silk ribbon (page 76)
- 4mm silk ribbon
- Chenille #22 needle

Leaves:
- Ribbon stitch (page 77)
- 4mm silk ribbon
- Chenille #22 needle

Stem and leaf detail:
- Stab/straight stitch (page 73)
- 1 strand DMC thread
- Milliners #7 needle

Small Beaded Bee with Organza Ribbon Wings

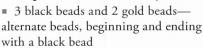

Body:
- Beaded backstitch (page 80)
- Nymo thread
- Beading needle

Bead placement for bee body:
- 3 black beads and 2 gold beads— alternate beads, beginning and ending with a black bead

Wings:
- Stab stitch (page 79)
- 7mm organza ribbon
- Chenille #22 needle

Round Spider Web

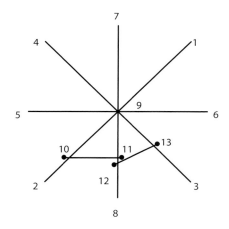

- Stab/straight stitch (page 73)
- Metallic thread
- Chenille #22 needle

1. I find the only way to create a good web is to work in a hoop.

2. Bring the needle to the surface of the work at 1. Make a long stab/straight stitch and reinsert at 2. Pull the thread taut and form an anchoring stitch. Cut the thread. Begin with a new strand of thread for each stab/straight stitch and each round. Come to the surface of the work at 3. Make a long stab/straight stitch and reinsert at 4. Pull thread taut and form an anchoring stitch. Continue until you have the desired number of spokes.

3. Bring the needle to the surface of the work in the center of the web at 9, and make a small holding stitch, securing all the threads where they meet. Bring the needle to the surface of the work to the left of a spoke, a small distance away from the center, at 10. Make a stab/straight stitch over the next 2 spokes on the right-hand side and reinsert at 11. Emerge on the left-hand side of the second spoke (in line with where the thread emerged) at 12, and make a stab/straight stitch over the next 2 spokes to 13. Continue until a round of web has been completed. Repeat until you have made the desired number of rounds.

Spider

Remember that spiders have very long legs, and 8 of them.

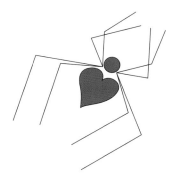

Head and body:
- Single-bead stitch (page 85)
- Nymo thread
- Milliners #10 needle

Legs:
- Stab/straight stitch (page 73)
- Metallic thread
- Chenille #22 needle

Straight Spider Web

- Stab/straight stitch (page 73)
- Metallic thread
- Chenille #22 needle

1. Bring the needle to the surface of the work at 1. Make a long stab/straight stitch and reinsert at 2. Pull thread taut and form an anchoring stitch. Cut the thread. Begin with a new thread for each stab/straight stitch and for each round. Bring the needle to the surface of the work again at 1. Make a long stab/straight stitch, angling away from the first spoke. Reinsert at 3 and form an anchoring knot. Continue until you have the desired number of spokes.

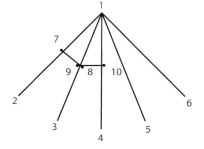

2. Bring the needle to the surface of the work a short distance from the point, at 7. Make a stab/straight stitch over the 2 spokes on the right and reinsert at 8. Emerge on the left-hand side of the second spoke, at 9. Make a stab/straight stitch over the next 2 spokes and reinsert at 10. Continue until you have the desired number of rounds.

Bow Button

- Button
- 4mm silk ribbon
- Chenille #22 needle

1. Insert the ribbon into a hole of the button from the right side of the work.

2. Do not pull the ribbon all the way through; leave enough ribbon to tie a small bow.

3. Come up through the adjacent hole to the surface of the work.

4. Tie a small bow on the surface of the button.

Button

Use the thread or ribbon to cover the Nymo thread on the attached button.

- Button
- Perle cotton #8 thread or 4mm silk ribbon

Button Cluster

- Buttons
- Beads
- Nymo thread
- Milliners #10 needle

1. It is very important that each button be stitched down separately to prevent the fabric from puckering under the buttons.

2. Tuck buttons under each other to create a compact cluster.

3. Embellish the buttons as desired.

Charm

- Charm
- Nymo thread
- Milliners #10 needle

1. Choose a Nymo thread that will blend with both the charm and the fabric that it is being attached to.

2. Sew on the charm, making the thread as invisible as possible.

Couched Braid or Trim

- Nymo thread
- Milliners #10 needle

1. To attach braid or trim, simply couch down with a matching Nymo thread in areas of the braid or trim so that the stitch will not be seen.

2. Embellish with beads, sequins, or colonial knots (page 71) as desired.

Couched Ribbon Garland

1. Any form of ribbon may be used with this technique.

2. With a length of ribbon, form gentle twists and turns on the surface of the work.

- Ribbon
- Nymo thread
- Chenille #22 and milliners #10 needles

3. Anchor the folds and twists with colonial knots (page 71) or single beads (page 85).

Couched Rickrack

1. Couch rickrack to the surface of the work with colonial knots (page 71), single beads (page 85), or stab/straight stitches (page 73).

- Rickrack
- Thread of choice
- Chenille #22 or milliners #7 needle

2. The tips of the rickrack may be couched with stab/straight stitches (page 73), lazy daisy/detached chain stitches (page 72), or pistil stitches (page 73).

Free-Form Flower with Beaded Center

1. Thread needle with a Nymo thread to match the ribbon.

- 11mm silk ribbon and Nymo thread
- Milliners #10 needle

2. Make a knot at the end of the thread.

3. Starting at an end of the ribbon, make small running stitches along the bottom edge.

4. Gather the ribbon to form a flower.

5. Stitch several times over the base of the flower so the gathers can't pull out.

6. Stitch the flower to the desired seam.

7. Add beads at the center of the flower.

Knotted Couched Ribbon

1. Tie soft knots in the desired length of 7mm silk ribbon.

- 7mm silk ribbon and Nymo thread
- Chenille #22 and milliners #10 needles

2. Couch the ribbon onto the work in the centers of the knots.

3. Keep the tension of the ribbon relaxed.

Layered Buttons

Lay a button on top of another to create texture and color.

- Buttons
- Nymo thread
- Milliners #10 needle

Simple Beaded Button

1. Come to the surface of the button through a hole.

- Button
- Beads
- Nymo thread
- Milliners #10 needle

2. Pick up as many beads as necessary to cover the space between the 2 holes.

3. Reinsert the needle and anchor firmly on the wrong side of the work.

Single-Bead Button

1. Come to the surface of the button through a hole.

- Button
- Beads
- Nymo thread
- Milliners #10 needle

2. Pick up a single bead large enough to cover the hole.

3. Reinsert into the same hole. Secure with an anchoring knot.

4. Repeat for the adjacent hole.

Stab-Stitch Couching

- 4mm and 7mm silk ribbon
- Chenille #22 needle

1. Lay the 7mm silk ribbon on the desired seam.

2. Using the 4mm silk ribbon, stab stitch (page 79) over the 7mm ribbon.

3. Allow the ribbon to fan out between the couching stitches.

4. This technique may also be used on other forms of trim, such as rayon tape.

Tied Button

1. Insert the thread or ribbon into a hole of the button from the right side of the work.

- Button
- 2mm silk ribbon, 4mm silk ribbon, or perle cotton #8 thread
- Chenille #22 or milliners #4 needle

2. Do not pull ribbon or thread all the way through.

3. Come up through the adjacent hole to the surface of the work.

4. Tie a knot on the surface of the button.

5. Trim the silk ribbon or thread to the desired length.

Finishing and Joining the Hexagons

Finishing supplies

Requirements for Completing and Joining Hexagons

- Embellished 4″ hexagons

- 4″ hexagon of Pellon 987F Fusible Fleece or Vilene H630 or equivalent lightweight fusible fleece

- 5″ taffeta (or backing fabric) hexagon

- Black sewing thread

- #8 perle cotton thread

- #4 and #7 milliners needles

- Small bulldog (binder) clips

- Rotary cutter, ruler, and mat

- Scissors

- Fluffy towel

- Iron and ironing board

> **NOTE**
> Hexagon sizing is based on the length of one side. Therefore, a 4″ hexagon has 6 sides that are each 4″ long.

Method

1. Lay the hexagon, embellished side up, on a cutting mat. Cut along the perimeter line of the hexagon (which was machine stitched at the beginning of the piecing stage).

2. Lay the hexagon, embellished side down, onto a folded towel. Lay the fusible fleece on it with the fusible side down. Carefully press until the fleece has adhered to the back of the hexagon.

3. Lay the backing hexagon, right side down, on a work surface. Center the embellished hexagon, right side up, on the backing hexagon. (The backing fabric should be 1″ larger than the embellished hexagon all the way around).

Center finished hexagon onto backing fabric.

4. Working on a side at a time of the hexagon, trim the backing fabric back to ¾″.

Trim backing fabric to ¾″.

5. Fold the backing fabric in half, so the raw edge aligns with the raw edge of the embellished hexagon. Finger press.

Fold backing fabric in half.

6. Fold the backing fabric again. It now lies folded over the embellished hexagon with the raw edges enclosed.

7. Use the small bulldog clips to hold the fabric in place.

Use small bulldog clips to hold fabric in place (hexagon).

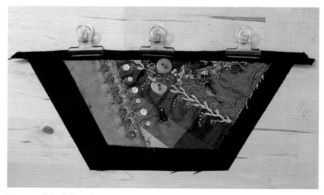

Use small bulldog clips to hold fabric in place (half-hexagon).

8. Stitch down the folded edge of backing fabric using a blind hem or appliqué stitch. Continue working on a side at a time (trimming the backing hexagon to ¾″ and stitching down the folded edge) until all raw edges of the hexagon are covered by the backing fabric.

9. Feather stitch around the hexagon with a perle cotton #8 thread of your choice.

10. Select the placement of the hexagons.

11. With the right sides facing each other, join the hexagons with a closely worked whipstitch.

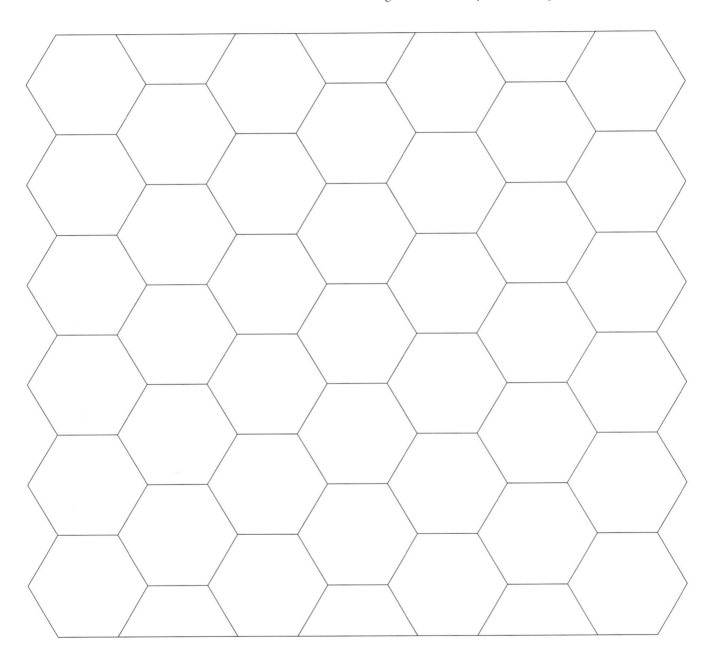

Voilà! Your personal crazy hexagon quilt is complete. I hope you enjoyed the trip!

12 Gallery

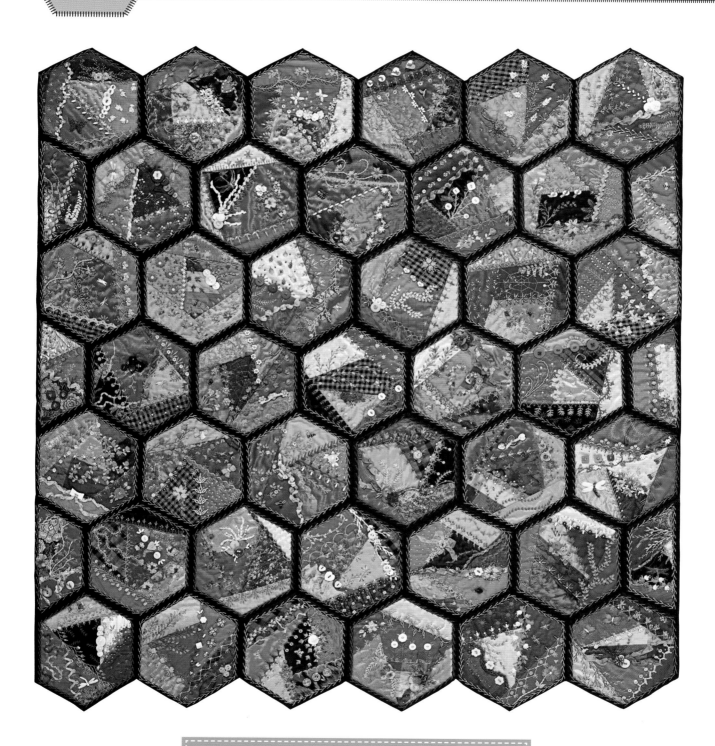

Crazy Hexagon Quilt

Colors of Africa Crazy Quilt

Crazy Victorian-Style Wallhanging

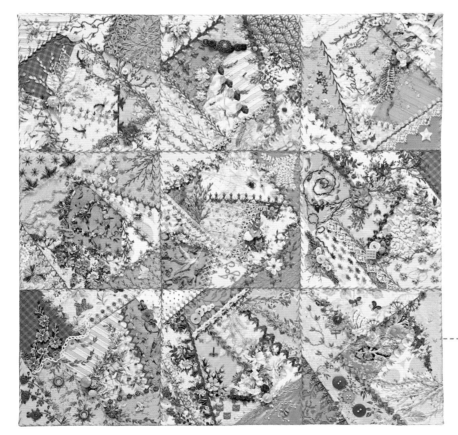

Pretty in Pink Crazy Quilt

Crazy Sewing Bag

Crazy Boxed Bag

Crazy Handbag

Crazy Spring Flower Bag

Crazy Vintage
Doily Tea Cozy

Crazy
Trinket Box

Patterns

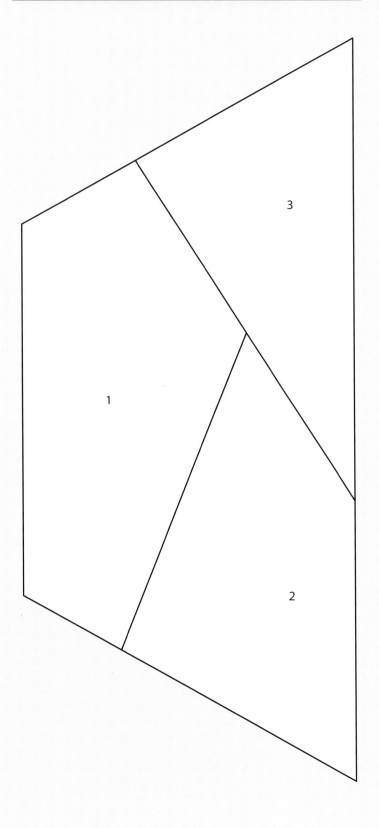

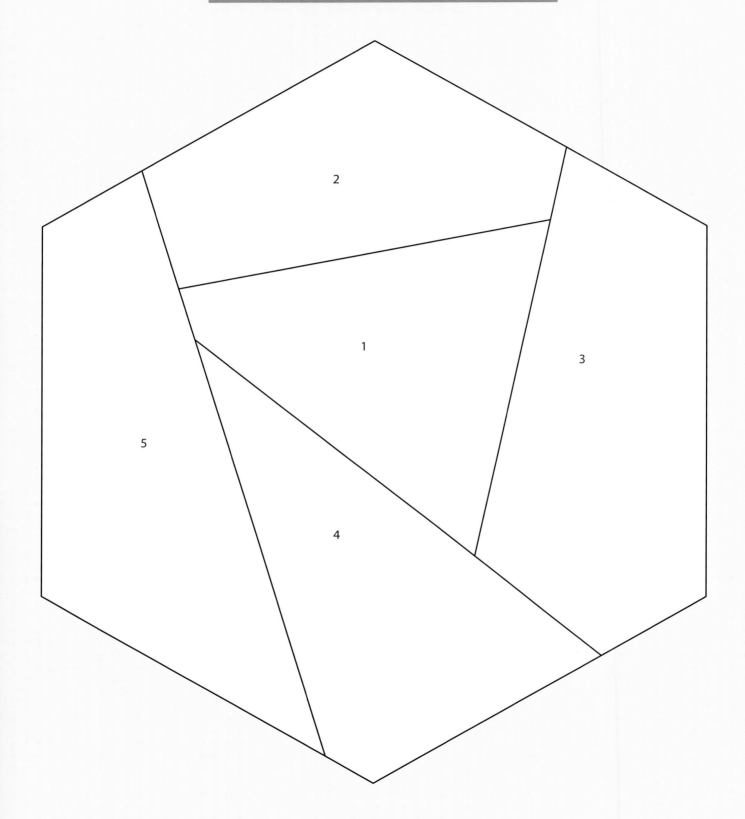

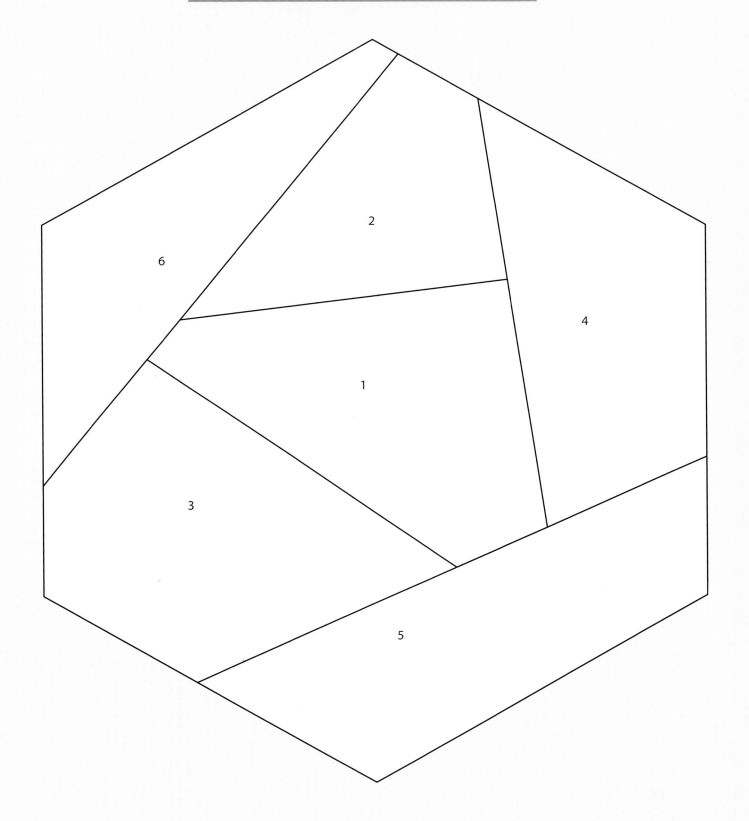

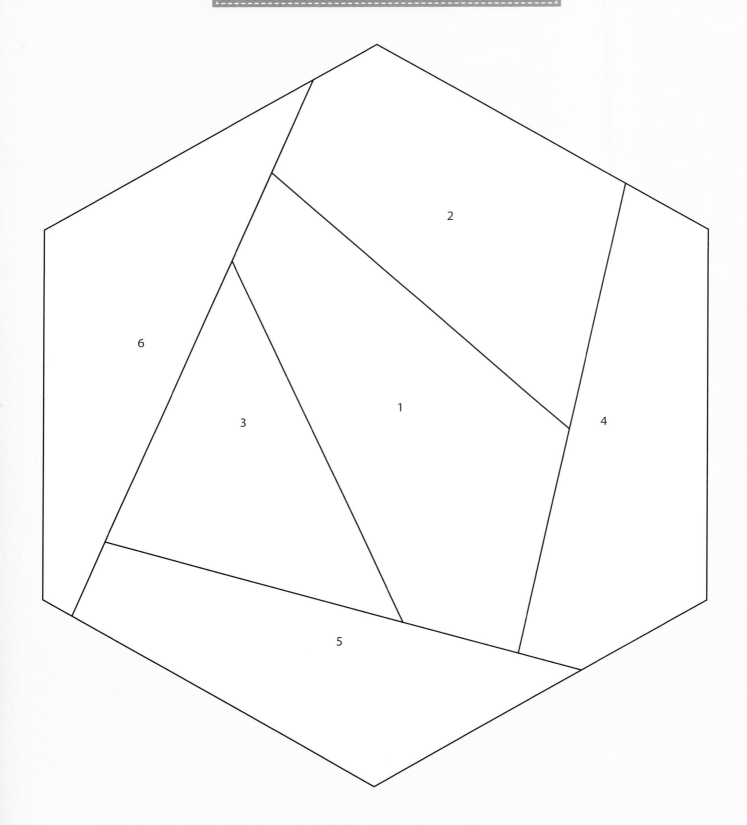

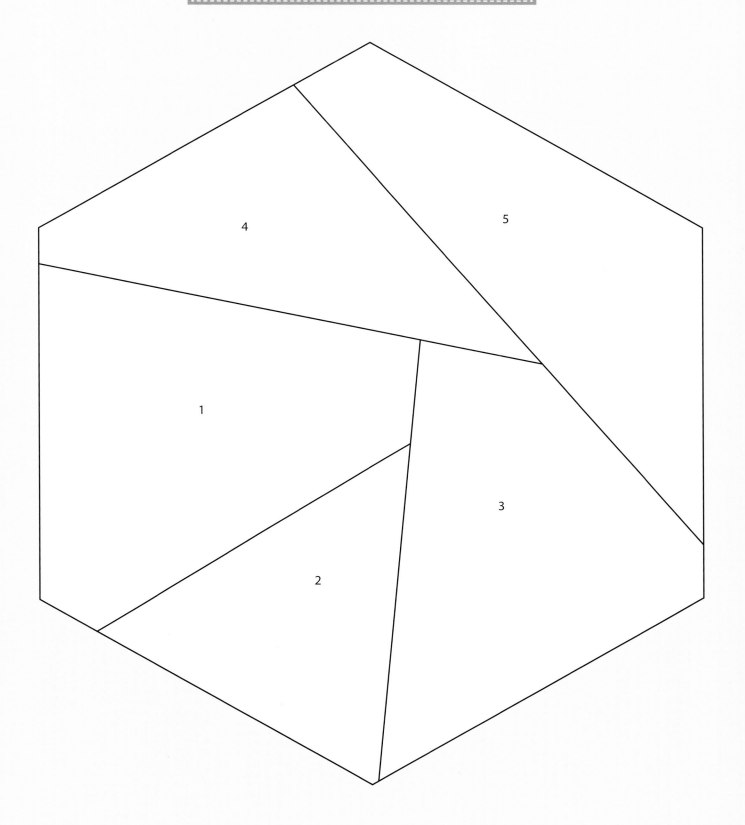

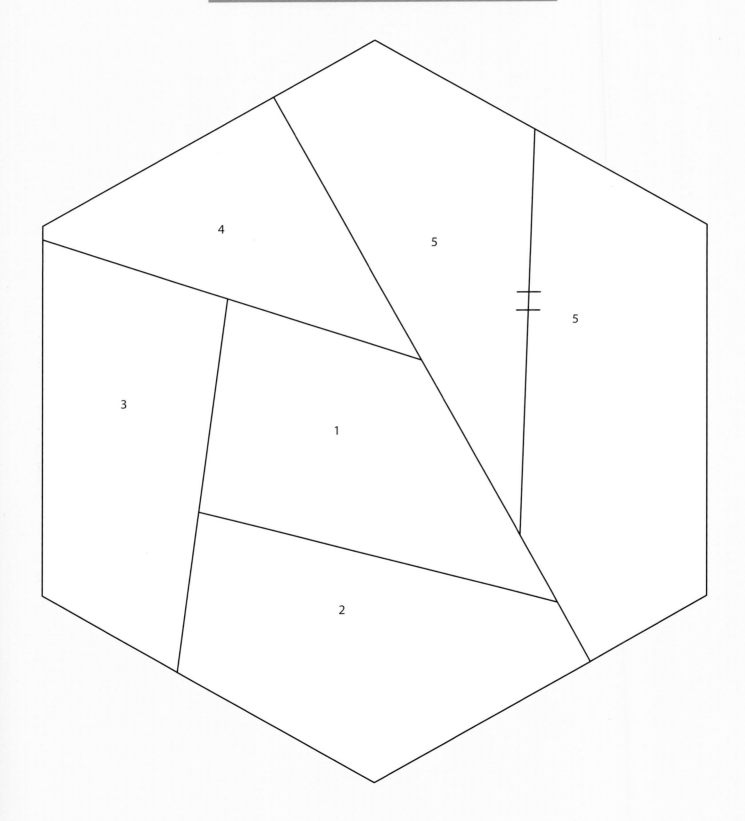

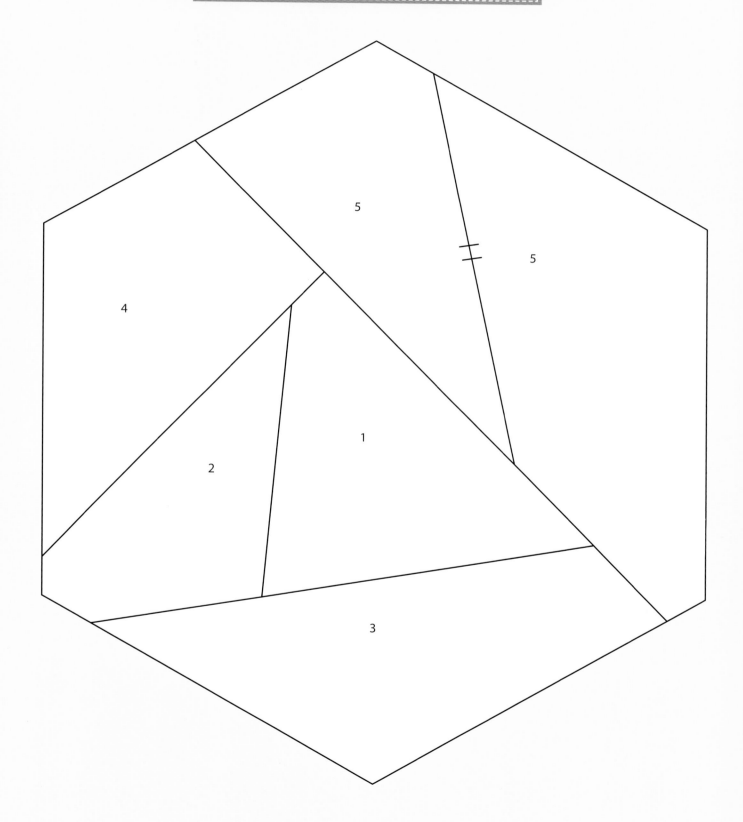

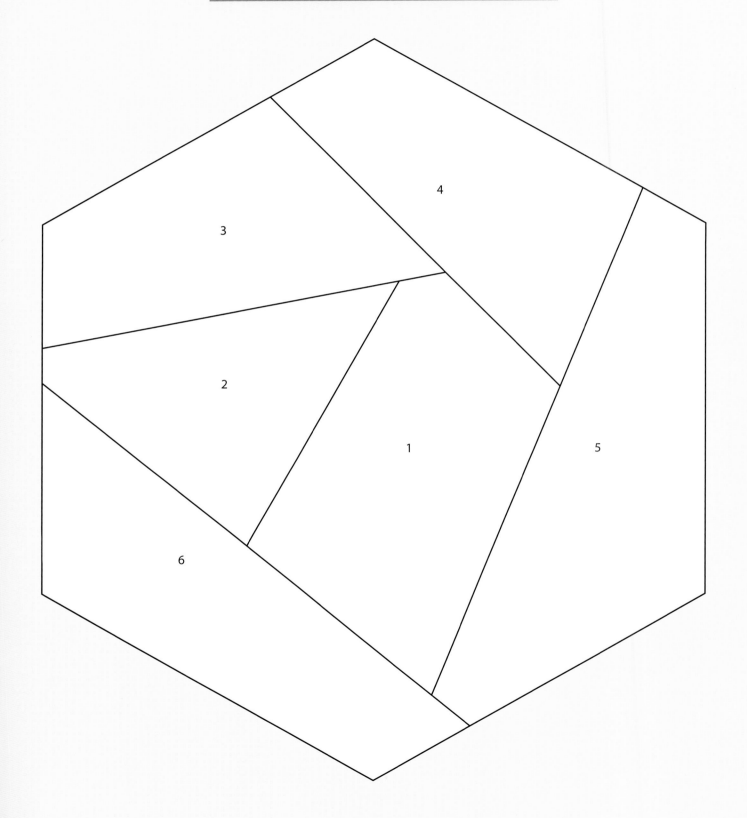

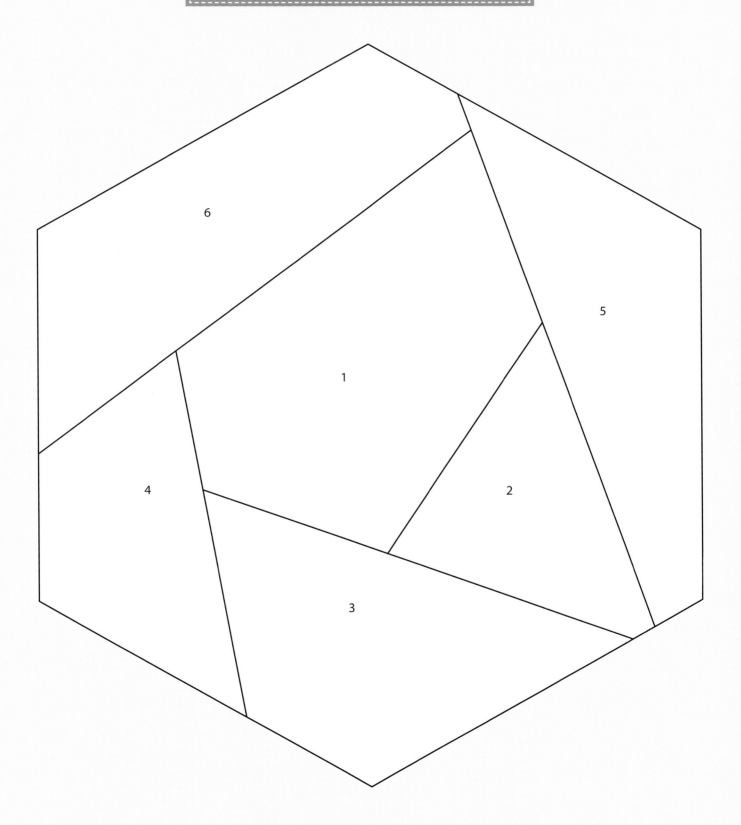

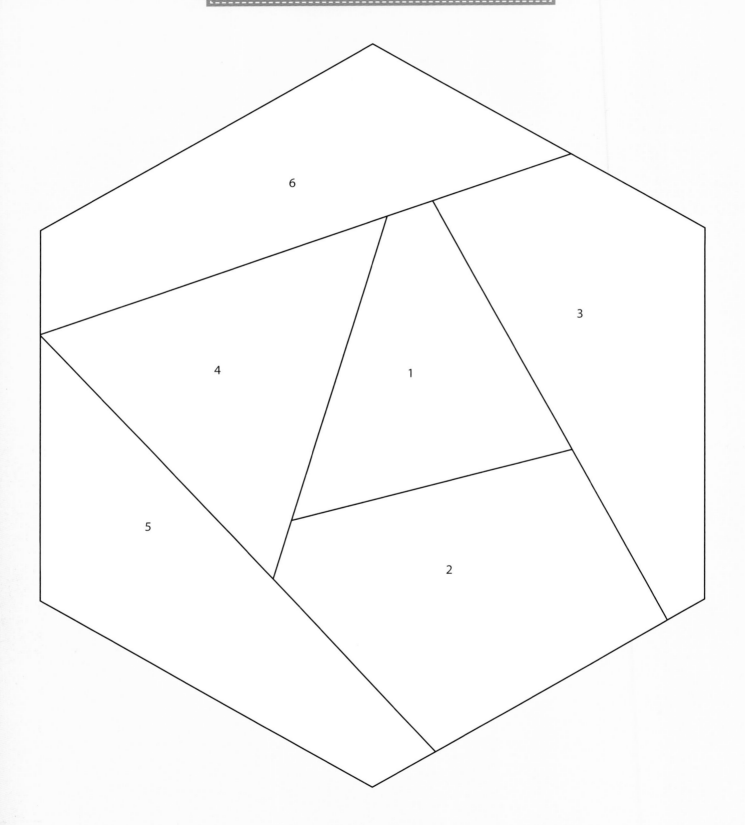

About the Author

Jenny Clouston lives on the beautiful Sunshine Coast in Queensland, Australia. She shares her home with her husband, Vaughn; two small white dogs, George and Gemsquash; and Charlotte, the cat. Her two adult children, Gareth and Ainslie, have recently flown the nest.

Her quilting journey began in her home country of South Africa and continued in Australia when she immigrated with her family in 2002.

The colors and culture of South Africa are a strong and underlying influence in her work.

Jenny is passionate about her craft and is willing to share her knowledge and skills within the quilting community. She currently teaches more than 45 students locally, who share her passion for the craft.

Jenny has a love for hand quilting, English paper piecing, and traditional quilts and their history.

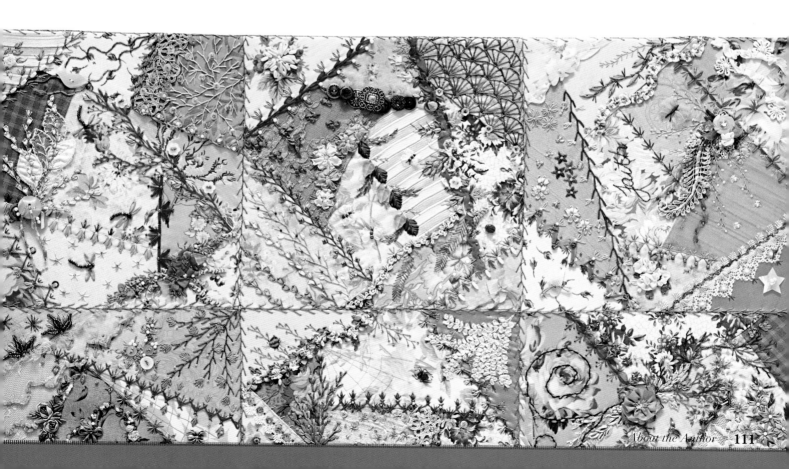

Great Titles and Products

from C&T PUBLISHING *and* stashBOOKS.

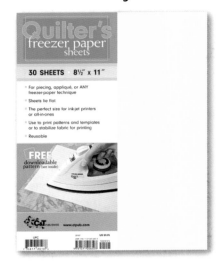

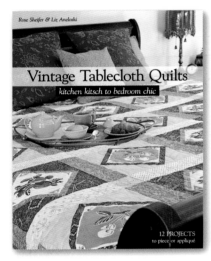

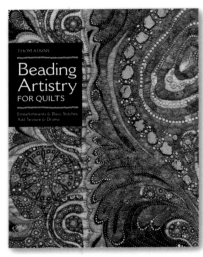

Available at your local retailer or **www.ctpub.com** *or* **800-284-1114**

For a list of other fine books from C&T Publishing, visit our website
to view our catalog online.

C&T PUBLISHING, INC.
P.O. Box 1456
Lafayette, CA 94549
800-284-1114

Email: ctinfo@ctpub.com
Website: www.ctpub.com

C&T Publishing's professional photography services are now available to
the public. Visit us at www.ctmediaservices.com.

Tips and Techniques can be found at www.ctpub.com > Consumer
Resources > Quiltmaking Basics: Tips & Techniques for Quiltmaking & More

For quilting supplies:

COTTON PATCH
1025 Brown Ave.
Lafayette, CA 94549
Store: 925-284-1177
Mail order: 925-283-7883

Email: CottonPa@aol.com
Website: www.quiltusa.com

Note: Fabrics shown may not be currently available, as fabric
manufacturers keep most fabrics in print for only a short time.